COMPELLED TO CRIME

Paternalism + DV and it right
to yeal wife

Domestic Violence - History
- when did Family pressure
become criminalize o
- or taste for Police.
- study in 1990's current v. movement

Battered Woman syndrome as a defense?

COMPELLED TO CRIME

*The Gender Entrapment of Battered
Black Women*

Beth E. Richie

ROUTLEDGE   New York • London

Published in 1996 by
Routledge
270 Madison Ave,
New York NY 10016

Published in Great Britain by
Routledge
2 Park Square, Milton Park,
Abingdon, Oxon, OX14 4RN

Transferred to Digital Printing 2010

Copyright ©1996 by Routledge

Book Design: Omega Clay
Cover Model: Coleen P. Stevens

Library of Congress Cataloging-in-Publication Data
Richie, Beth.
    Compelled to crime: the gender entrapment of battered Black
women / by Beth E. Richie.
            p.   cm.
    Includes bibliographical references and index.
    ISBN 0-415-91144-3 (HB). — ISBN 0-415-91145-1 (pbk.)
    1. Afro-American women—Abuse of—New York (N.Y.)—Case
studies. 2. Abused women—New York (N.Y.)—Interviews.
I. Title.
HV6626.22.N7R53 1995
362.82′92′0899601307471—dc20   95-18322
                                                          CIP

Publisher's Note
The publisher has gone to great lengths to ensure the quality of this reprint
but points out that some imperfections in the original may be apparent.

CONTENTS

ACKNOWLEDGMENTS

AMONG other things, the women who shared their life histories with me taught me that we are able to face the challenges, endure the hardships and accomplish our life goals because of the good people around us. Surrounding me during the research and writing of this book were many wise, strong women and supportive men. I gratefully acknowledge their contributions to this book.

Professors Catherine Silver, Leith Mullings, and Judith Lorber, the chair of my dissertation committee, guided my initial intellectual journey to Rikers Island. Each of these feminist scholars, in their own way, influenced my academic growth far beyond the scope of this research. Their commitment to me and this project were essential elements of its successful completion.

I am blessed to work with students and faculty who strive to make a difference in the world. My associates at Hunter College of the City University of New York took an active interest in and offered tremendous support for my work on this book. The ways they blend activism and academics provide important models for me. The staff of the Health Link Project of the Hunter College Center on AIDS, Drugs and Community Health were inspirational and instructive colleagues, as were several employees of the Montefiore Rikers Island Health Services who facilitated my access to the Rose M. Singer Jail and the women detained there.

The fine people who work in the communities where most of the people detained at Rikers Island come from are among those whom I honor and appreciate most. There are many committed women and grassroots organizations who tirelessly work in the movement to end violence against women, and working with them for the past twenty years has inspired me and shaped my thinking. They have shown how important it is to struggle every day to make a difference, and I take strength from their passionate persistence and their optimistic vision that things can, indeed, change. The women at VIP (The Violence Intervention Project) in East Harlem, New York have been some of the best teachers in my life. Much of what I know is because of knowing them. Members of CLAIM (Chicago Legal Aid to Incarcerated Mothers) opened their doors to me and let me sit with them in support groups as they responded daily to the complexities associated with being released from prison. Sue Ostoff at the National Clearinghouse for the Defense of Battered Women and Gail Garfield at the Institute to Research and Respond to Violence in the Lives of African American Women have not only contributed to how I came to understand gender entrapment, but they are changing how the world understands African American battered women and women involved in illegal activities in this difficult political time.

For one wonderful year while writing this book I lived in Chicago, Illinois. As a visiting scholar at The Center For Research on Women and Gender at the University of Illinois at Chicago I was supported by funding from the MacArthur Foundation. Alice J. Dan, Zylphia Ford, Vanessa Aubert, Mary Lynn Dietsche and several graduate students not only provided general support for my work, but they took particular interest in the final production details of this book—those that typically only an author would care about. For the space to work and the best feminist companionship a visitor could ask for, I thank them deeply.

My editor, Jayne Fargnoli, and her colleagues at Routledge demonstrated how much they cared about this book by guiding the manuscript through the editorial and production process with thoughtful attention to every detail. They demonstrated tremendous respect for me as an author. Even more importantly, they respected the women whose stories are told in this book.

The book would never have been written without the support of my families. My family of choice, Catlin Fullwood, Suzanne Pharr and Jane B. Jacobs took my work very seriously but never let me take myself too seriously. Elsa A. Rios has helped me be brave and honest in sharing my ideas, and provided the sense of perspective and history that grounded my work. A. Jamie Jiménez brought joy and distraction just when I needed them. She was patient and kind about my obsession with this book during the final days of writing. Jamie understands and appreciates me as a writer and she taught me many things about myself as a woman. Dana Ain Davis paid attention to the mundane details of the manuscript and never lost sight of the overall story of gender entrapment that I was trying to tell. When I had my doubts, she reminded me that I *could* write a book and that I *must write this one.* It was Valli Kanuha who listened to the ideas in the very beginning. She thought through conceptual and methodological dilemmas with keen insight and edited various drafts of the manuscript. She believed in this book at every moment, and offered gentle, loving support at the turn of every page. It was Val who sent me flowers in the end.

I come from people, my family of origin, whose proud Black traditions, strong loyalty, and deep sense of justice set the foundation for this work. My grandparents, Ruth A. Jourdain, Henry M. Jourdain, Celeste Richie, William F. Richie, along with the others before them, cleared the path for my life. I stood humbly on their shoulders as I wrote this book.

My sisters, Laurel J. Richie, Anne Richie Hohl and Charlotte Golar Richie, my brothers Winston H. Richie and Louis Hohl, my nieces and nephews, and my Aunt Janet Richie Whitiker, formed a close web of support around me while I worked. Winston and Anne called often, while Laurel shared coffee, confidences, and copyediting suggestions. They each know that I believe that while it may be chance that made us brothers and sisters, it is the love we share so openly that makes them my best friends. Their companionship kept me laughing and living well while I studied and wrote.

My parents Beatrice J. Richie and Winston H. Richie gave generous amounts of optimism, praise, and encouragement to keep me going through the writing of this book. As always, they provided the kind of family love that gave home to my heart. I've learned that a family home for the heart is a *very* important asset to have when writing a book about painful and distressing circumstances. I am blessed to have these various families who care deeply about me and understand my passion for this work.

There was one very special muse whose life inspired me at the most trying moments during this project. Elisabeth Mason Hopkins's life reminds me that having a chance to work hard toward something that I believe in is, after all, a privilege. Her life taught me that I have a responsibility to use my privilege well.

I learn most of what I know and write about from listening carefully to battered and incarcerated women tell their stories. My life history will forever be changed by the lessons the thirty–seven women at Rikers Island taught me; they are among the most generous souls that I have known. I hope that this book will dignify them by contributing to our society understanding better who they are. In the end, I've written it believing that with a better understanding, more of us will feel compelled to confront the deadly conditions of institutionalized racism, persistent poverty and violence.

I respectfully dedicate this book to the women whose stories are told in it, and the countless other women who are incarcerated because they were compelled to crime by the violence in their lives. May the future bring a world with more understanding, and safety, and more justice.

COMPELLED TO CRIME

I

INTRODUCTION

*"They can tell that their mama is not like other mothers.
They can see that she is working hard to give them more
than food, shelter, and clothes to wear; that she wants to
give them a taste of the delicious, a vision of beauty, a bit
of ecstasy. Even so, she is obsessed with the latest products.
She is moving away from her awareness of the deeper inner
things of life and worrying about money. I watch these
changes in her and worry. I want her never to lose what she
has given me—a sense that there is something deeper, more
to this life than the everyday."*
               —bell hooks, "Reflections of a 'Good' Daughter" [1]

EVERY DAY in this country some women are co-
erced or forced by circumstances into doing things they don't
want to do. For many women, it is the only static condition of
their ever changing lives: to regularly feel required to make hard
choices among, at times, very poor options.

This situation forces some of us to assume a posture in the
world that isn't in our best interest, or we betray ourselves for
the good of others by acting in ways or living in relationships
that don't serve us well. Others of us feel compelled to cut deals
to protect our safety, or we compromise our integrity to secure
sufficient resources to provide for ourselves and our families.
Constrained by threatening circumstances, we withhold the
truth of our lives, deferring our dreams and ignoring our desires
in order to get the basic things that we need to survive.

This book is a collection of women's stories whose lives
vividly illustrate this condition. Their everyday existence has
been shaped by very threatening circumstances, many deferred
dreams, tremendous unmet needs, and exceptionally hard choices. And yet, their stories represent only the most extreme version of that which is a very common experience for women: being controlled and feeling constrained by tense intimate re-

lationships within a hostile social world. The extent to which some women experience this predicament is directly related to the degree of stigma, isolation, and marginalization imposed by their social position. The choices are harder and the consequences are more serious for women with low incomes, women of color, lesbians, women who become pregnant at a young age, and others whose decisions, circumstances, and status violate the dominant culture's expectations or offend hegemonic images of "womanhood."

The cases presented here are extreme not because the *women themselves* are extreme, but because the degree to which *their lives* are stigmatized and marginalized is extreme. They are African American women from low–income communities who are physically battered, sexually assaulted, emotionally abused, and involved in illegal activity. Their stories vividly contradict the popular impression—perpetuated by mainstream social scientists, human service providers, public policy analysts and legislators—that the escalating rates of violence against women, poverty, addiction and women's participation in crime is because of women's psychological, moral, or social inadequacies. Increasingly, women's problems in contemporary society are blamed on individual character flaws: women are considered masochistic, with self–defeating personality disorders, confused in their decision–making, unable to solve serious problems.

However, the stories in this book illustrate the contrary. To a significant extent, the devastated and deteriorating position of some women in contemporary society is a socially constructed condition. Poor African American battered women in contemporary society are increasingly restricted by their gender roles, stigmatized by their racial/ethnic and class position, and constrained by the competing forces of tremendous unmet need and very limited resources. This predicament leaves them facing complicated ethical, moral, and practical dilemmas. The women feel pushed and pulled by their basic survival needs, their expectations of themselves, and others' requirements of them. In the end, *despite* their various attempts to conform to the standard gender roles, *despite* their efforts to follow the cultural mores of their racial/ethnic community, and *despite* their interest in obeying the social rules, women like those in this book are structurally and situationally unable to meet competing and sometimes contradictory demands of contemporary social life.

These women's stories will show the extent to which our society has set up this situation. Society has been organized in such a manner that some women are almost destined to fail; they quite simply *cannot* succeed in the current social arrangements. Obviously, one could argue that conformity to hegemonic standards of gender roles is less than desirable, and that indeed it is the social arrangements that need to change. This is precisely the conclusion I will come to in this book. However, unlike the body of feminist scholarship that advocates the unilateral abolition of gender roles as an organizing construct, it must be understood that despite the *advantages* of alternative identities and lifestyles *for some women*, for most low–income women of color, existing outside of the dominant society and non–conformity with the mainstream is *not* a privileged position or a viable option. In fact, for the women whose stories are told here, it is precisely *because* of their deep interest in fitting in and their attempts to succeed that their failures are mistakenly attributed to their individual shortcomings rather than social conditions. This is how they were set up; left with no good, safe way to avoid the problematic social circumstances that they find themselves in, unable to change their social position, and ultimately blamed for both. I call this set–up—this extreme situation—gender entrapment.

The notion of gender entrapment came to me one day in May of 1992 when I walked into the Rose M. Singer Center, the women's jail at Rikers Island Correctional Facility. There, on any given day, approximately 2,000 women are detained under the auspices of the New York City Department of Corrections. By far, the majority of the detainees are women of color from low–income communities. Over fifty percent are African American. While the "official" sources report that at least half of the women there are battered women, my experience as an activist and advocate in anti–violence programs had me convinced that far more than that have been abused by their partners.[2]

What I had *not* anticipated when I began going to Rikers Island was the extent to which physical assaults, emotional degradation, marginalized/tenuous economic status and overt racism formed a seemingly impermeable web of despair around the African American battered women in the jail. Nor did I expect to find such stories of resistance, resolve and respectability. For despite the seemingly overwhelming circumstances, the lives of the African American battered women I met at Rikers Island Correctional Facility reflected a complex dualism; they are at once victims and survivors, inspiring and overwhelmed, courageous and terrified, sometimes engaged social actors and other times passive witnesses to the oppressive chaos around them.

The gender entrapment theoretical paradigm is an attempt to illuminate this dialectic—the contradictions and complications of the lives of the African American battered women who commit crimes—by explaining the link between culturally constructed gender–identity development, violence against women in intimate relationships, and women's participation in illegal activities. Gender entrapment is my attempt to describe the social process that links them as a theoretical explanation of battered women's involvement in crime.

The term gender entrapment appropriates its meaning from the legal notion of entrapment, which implies a circumstance whereby an individual is lured into a compromising act. When applied to African American battered women who commit crimes, I use gender entrapment to describe the socially constructed process whereby African American women who are vulnerable to men's violence in their intimate relationship are penalized for behaviors they engage in even when the behaviors are logical extensions of their racialized gender identities, their culturally expected gender roles, and the violence in their intimate relationships. The model illustrates how gender, race/ethnicity, and violence can intersect to create a subtle, yet profoundly effective system of organizing women's behavior into patterns that leave women vulnerable to private and public subordination, to violence in their intimate relationships and, in turn, to participation in illegal activities. As such, the gender–entrapment theory helps to explain how some women who participate in illegal activities do so in response to violence, the threat of violence, or coercion by their male partners.

Their stories illustrate how they were invisible to feminist anti–violence programs, ignored by mainstream social science, misunderstood by criminal justice policy analysts, and stigmatized by the general public because the nature of their abuse and their social position resulted in their being labeled "criminals" rather than "victims of crimes." More generally, the concept suggests how some women's everyday efforts to survive are not only discounted or invisible, but are increasingly *criminalized* in contemporary society.

The more I learned about the lives of the African American battered women in jail, the more I came to understand just how profoundly set up (or entrapped) they were. In the private sphere of their lives they were deeply misunderstood by the people closest to them, betrayed by their loyalty to their families and communities, and abused and degraded in their most intimate relationships. At the same time, they were trying desperately to exist in a social world that was determined to condemn them, only to be exiled from the broader society that failed to deliver promised opportunity and rewards. To this, add the social context of an unresponsive social service system, a meanspirited and repressive public welfare agenda, increasingly aggressive law enforcement policies, and growing social intolerance for women who cannot or do not "fit in" to dominant society... and their gender entrapment becomes clearer.

The women I met at Rikers Island Correctional Facility were detained there for various alleged criminal violations. However, through their stories I came to understand that they actually had been imprisoned at different points in their lives in other, more symbolic ways. They were confined by social conditions in their communities, restrained by their families' circumstances, severely limited by abuse in their intimate relationships, and forced to make hard choices with very few options. As such, they were imprisoned well before they were arrested and taken to Rikers Island, and not surprisingly, this earlier, more fundamental sense of confinement, is strikingly similar to the conditions of being in jail today.

These earlier, more formative restraints re–emerge in striking ways within the walls that imprison the women at Rikers Island Correctional Facility. Rikers Island is one of the largest detention centers in the United States. More than 125,000 people come through it every year, with an average daily census of more than 16,000. More than eighty percent of inmates in custody of New York City jails are detainees awaiting adjudication: to be found guilty or innocent of the charge for which they were arrested. The remainder are incarcerated because they violated their parole, were convicted of a misdemeanor and sentenced to less than one year in a city jail, or were convicted of a felony and await transfer to the New York state prison system.[3]

Similar to the national trend, the women's population on Rikers Island has risen precipitously in the last few years. In 1987, women made up seven percent of the inmate population; presently, they constitute twelve percent of the population, an average daily census of 2,000. In the last three years, the number of women incarcerated at Rikers Island has doubled. The women who make up the population typically are women of color who live in New York City's most destitute neighborhoods, where violence, poverty, and lack of health and human services have come to symbolize the institutionalized racism and governmental neglect of inner cities in this country.

At Rikers, the women are subject to demeaning procedures that reflect their marginalized position in the "free world." They enter the facility through the receiving area, where they wait in small cells to be showered and given a routine medical screening. The physical arrangements allow for virtually no privacy: the cells are barred on three sides, with a steel toilet in one corner. "New admissions" must surrender their clothing and don hospital gowns or, when supplies run short, wrap themselves in cotton bedsheets or harsh woolen blankets. The women describe the process of being arrested and incarcerated as extremely traumatic. Arrests are usually unexpected, interrupting the activities of daily life: work or other income–producing activities, caring for children or meeting family responsibilities, and, indeed, being arrested interrupts the criminal activity. The women usually arrive at Rikers Island exhausted, upset, and sick after being held in police custody for up to thirty-six hours. During that time they are indicted and charged, and bail is set—a process characterized by long periods of waiting and by having to respond to police, court, and correctional officers, typically male, who treat the women inmates with disgust and contempt. When the women are arrested, their identities abruptly shift from "free persons" to "detainees," effectively stripping them of even the limited rights, privileges, privacy, and respect they may have been accorded on the outside.

Once admitted to the jail, the women are assigned to one of two basic types of inmate housing based on space availability (and Rikers is usually overcrowded), the nature of the women's charge, and their health status, including pregnancy, communicable diseases, and mental health problems.

Depending on the woman's classification, based on factors such as their charge, age, health status, and prior record, as an inmate they are entitled to a variety of services. However, the availability of these services changes based on conditions in the jail, the sentiment of current elected officials, and the philosophy of the Department of Corrections administration. The correctional system's goal of custody, confinement, and control takes precedence over delivering services, and in reality, daily life for women at Rikers Island is monotonous, rigidly controlled and tense. With rare exceptions, the women detained in the Rose M. Singer Center spend their time anxiously waiting for their court dates with very little information or support and few distractions. They fill their time watching television, playing cards, talking with one another, anticipating their next visit from families, and sometimes trying to get into a program or making an appointment for social service assistance. Since movement within the facility is regulated, accomplishing even a small task, such as keeping follow-up appointments for daily medication, is difficult.

The amount of idle time has important consequences for daily life at Rikers Island. While in detention, the women experience an extraordinary level of alienation, frustration, and depersonalization, as well as fear, apprehension, and powerlessness. Routine activities for women at Rikers Island are done in groups, including showering, eating, visiting relatives, or meeting with attorneys. Standards of behavior based on security needs are rigidly enforced. The women must stand or sit quietly before privileges are granted; they walk through the institution in lines, and very few conversations are confidential, despite professional "privileged communication" statutes. As inmates the women have come to expect very little privacy, an expectation that is reinforced by the spontaneous "raids" of their living spaces, along with bodily searches for contraband (hairpins, rubber bands, chewing gum, drugs, sharp instruments, etc.) and unpredictable alarms when all movement in the facility is halted for an indefinite period of time.

The loss of personal autonomy has important and lasting implications for women inmates' sense of identity. Most of them are known by the aliases they gave when they were arrested, by institutional nicknames, or by their identification numbers printed on plastic bracelets (like hospital bands) that they are required to wear on their wrists. Even their physical appearance is regulated. They are not legally required to wear institutional uniforms; however, if they choose to wear civilian clothing, they are allowed only two sets from the clothing bin. The clothes are often ill–fitting, unseasonal, and unsuited for institutional wear. The clothes are donated from used clothing programs, such as the Salvation Army, and are soiled and torn; shoes are likely to be mismatched. This has serious implications for how women inmates present themselves in court, with their families, or with others in the institution itself.

The most obvious and perhaps most serious institutional issue for women in jail on Rikers Island is the loss of freedom and privilege concomitant with arrest and incarceration. Immediately upon entry into the criminal justice system, they are reduced to a dependent, powerless status where authority is used indiscriminately, and humiliation or physical intimidation are common. By most accounts, the consequences of being arrested and incarcerated result in marginalization and feelings of alienation, even if the accused individual is acquitted. The detainee must ask for everyday items like toilet paper, and they must get permission for such simple, everyday activities as turning their lights on or off.

A telling symbol of the profound effect their lower status has on women at Rikers Island is that those who have "good" relationships with the officers refer to them as "mommy" or "daddy" (Mommy Smith, Daddy Jones). While this could be interpreted as a cultural expression connoting affection, it also illustrates how the women at Rikers Island have learned that the best way to interact with authorities in the institution is by bargaining for extra privileges through elevating the officers' status, and by seeking approval with a self–effacing demeanor, a childlike tone of voice, and, sometimes, a highly sexualized persona.

This book is the story of thirty–seven women at Rikers—and, I think, the stories of countless women like them. In vivid ways, their voices describe important and troubling dimensions of the human condition in contemporary society: their own words tell a very convincing story of gender entrapment.

I will use the remainder of this chapter to present the backdrop to their stories—describing the broader social context within which the women interviewed for this book live. Chapter Two is an elaboration on the research dimensions of the story. After presenting a demographic profile of the women I interviewed, I review the life history interview process I used to collect the stories.

The individual stories begin in Chapter Three where the women describe what it was like for them as children in their households and communities, where, as Beverly, age thirty–three, says, "growing up as a black girl was hard, but good." In Chapter Four, the women's experience of violence—the horrific degradation and their varied responses to it—will be shared, as they describe how they were "just trying to deal with the force of his blows" (Inca, age thirty–one). Reading these accounts will help readers understand the paths the women took to illegal activity, which are described in Chapter Five, when the women found themselves "running, dealing, robbing and stealing" (Aisha, age twenty–six). The concept of gender entrapment—how women were compelled to crime—becomes clearer as these and other women's stories unfold.

In Chapter Six, I return to the discussion of the broad social context and merge it with the women's stories. The aim here is to show in a more macroanalytic sense how the theoretical model of gender entrapment explains how some battered women were compelled to crime. In the final chapter I offer policy recommendations as a conclusion to the story of gender entrapment.

THE SOCIAL CONTEXT
OF GENDER ENTRAPMENT

In the past five years, three trends have paved the way for this exploration of the relationship among gender, race/ethnicity, violence, and crime. The criminal justice system has been altered significantly by the increase in women detained in correctional facilities; the grass–roots battered women's movement has found an audience in the mainstream public; and the social sciences have been challenged to expand the traditional academic discourse to include "minority voices," encouraging scholarship on the experiences of women and people of color.[4] These trends have raised compelling political, scholarly, and practical questions. Taken together, they provided the broader sociological context for the analysis of the life–history interviews that led to the theoretical model of gender entrapment.

The Limits of Scholarship

Like many other social scientists whose perspectives have been informed by grass–roots activism, I was exhilarated by the new scholarship on the intersection of race/ethnicity, gender, and class that was beginning to influence the social sciences. In particular, I was interested in feminist epistemological approaches to research on African American women and the Black family suggesting that accurate knowledge about an understudied, marginalized group requires that an "interested" standpoint be assumed.[5] Yet, while feminist scholars and others have developed psychological theories to explain gender inequality and the inferior position of women in contemporary society,[6] the majority of the theoretical and empirical work in the area of gender identity is not directly relevant to the majority of women detained on Rikers Island. It has not been adequately applied to theories of women's criminality, violence against women, or the institutional marginalization that women from disenfranchised communities experience.

Similarly, the "new race" scholarship, which looks at ethnic identity, has not typically focused on gender as a significant variable. As a result, crucial issues have gone unexplored, among them cultural variance in the expression of gender identity, the role of race/ethnicity and culture in the construction of gender roles, and the impact of institutionalized discrimination on African American women's gendered behavior.

Activism and Research on Violence Against Women

The second stimulus for conducting these interviews and writing this book was my interest in critiquing the burgeoning movement to end violence against women in which I had been a participant observer for fifteen years. The anti–violence movement for social change, motivated by the national statistic that indicates that at least twenty–five percent of all married women are battered by their male partners and at least half of all women relating to men in an intimate relationship will be assaulted at least once during the course of that relationship, was organized by feminist activists.[7] As a loosely formed network of feminist rape crisis programs, battered women's shelters, and grass–roots women's centers, the anti–violence movement has, in only twenty years, grown to constitute a distinct area of feminist activism and social-service program delivery in this country. Currently, at least six national and international organizations specifically address the issue of domestic violence, and more than 2,000 programs provide crisis–intervention services for battered women.

Violence against women has entered into public discourse as a pressing social problem, as reflected by the media attention to highly sensationalized and celebrity cases of sexual abuse and battering, as well as the proliferation of self–help books for abused women and "survivor's stories" of intimate violence. Significant political effort has gone into the passing of national legislation and state laws designed to more adequately protect women against violence in intimate relationships. Whereas prior to the mid–1970s, violence against women was considered a private aberration of family life, twenty years later many women now reach out for help from a vast array of available services, according to the National Coalition Against Domestic Violence and the National Domestic Violence Resource Center. However, despite these accomplishments, this grass–roots feminist movement has had limited success in creating the social changes necessary to end violence against women, partly because it has failed to address the needs of those whose lives are most marginalized.[8]

Similarly, the scholarly treatment and research on violence against women in intimate relationships has been limited by conceptual and methodological oversights.[9] The feminist critique of the research typically cites the vague categories used in the scales, and the limitation of culturally bound concepts that permeate the data collection instruments. The large-survey approaches, such as the National Crime Survey, are criticized for their tendency to underreport instances of abuse.[10] Even the most widely used instrument, the Conflict Tactics Scale (CTS), is considered limited because it counts acts of violence outside of the context within which they occur, and there is a noted lack of attention to the differential effects of the various acts of violence on the lives of the victim.

While all of these data collection instruments have helped legitimatize the study of abuse in intimate relationships, they are considered too quantitative and take the experiences of women out of context: the focus often is on the motivation for violent men's behavior—counting incidents rather than understanding dynamics or effects. The victim's perspective, if considered at all, is typically explored from a psychological rather than a social or institutional perspective. And those studies that have been conducted from the standpoint of the battered woman have been overwhelmingly concerned with the experiences of white women.[11] While there have been important and interesting new developments in the measurement of family violence, the flaws still exist.[12]

The aggregate effect is that while *some* battered women are safer in the 1990s than they were in the 1970s, and while we know more about *general* patterns in the population, we still have very little theoretical or empirical work that speaks to African American battered women from low–income communities. Consequently, few anti–violence programs, criminal justice policies, or theoretical explanations are sensitive to ethnic differences or address cultural issues that give particular meaning to violence in intimate relationships for African American or other women of color.[13] Furthermore, those whose lives are complicated by drug use, prostitution, illegal immigrant status, low literacy, and a criminal record continue to be misunderstood, underserved, isolated, and, as the stories in this book indicate, in serious physical and emotional danger.[14]

It is important for readers to note that I consider myself among the feminist activists who worked diligently to frame an analysis of violence against women that criminalize it. By likening it to other forms of assault, we believed that the issue would be taken more seriously by criminal justice authorities, social service providers and the general public. While many of us were leery of too much emphasis on criminal justice intervention as a solution, in retrospect we did not pay enough attention to the consequences of adopting the rhetoric that "violence against women is a crime." Though this helped lead to some important legal changes and shifts in public consciouness, what we did was categorically exclude women who were involved in illegal activity from the services they needed as battered women.

Women as Inmates

The third trend that inspired this book was the unprecedented social and political attention given to the problems of crime and violence in contemporary society. Public opinion polls indicate that most people in this country think of crime as *the* major social problem in the United States. Community forums and national conferences are dedicated to it, politicians win or lose elections because of their position on it, and prison–related goods and services are a major growth industry in this county. More stringent criminal justice policies—truth in sentencing, mandatory terms, and death penalty legislation—have become the concrete manifestations of the tough–on–crime public sentiment. Motivated by fear and reinforced by sensationalized, simplistic and stereotyped treatment of the issue by the mainstream media, this trend reflects a deepening tension between members of different social groups, intolerance of poor people, frustrations over persistent problems, a resurgence of racist hostility, and the backlash by conservative right–wing forces in this country.

A troubling dimension of this trend is the increasing rate of imprisonment of women in this country, especially low–income, African American women.[15] Each day 1,500 people enter jails or prisons in the United States, which has one of the highest incarceration rates in the world. According to the National Institute of Justice, the prison population is rising by thirteen percent each year, with women representing one of the fastest growing populations in criminal justice institutions. In 1980, for example, approximately 13,000 women were in federal and state prisons; by the end of 1989, that number had more than tripled. In 1989 alone, the female prison population increased by twenty-five percent, compared to a thirteen percent rise in the male prison population.

Criminal justice institutions include federal and state prisons, probation and parole systems, and nearly 3,000 county or municipal jails. As distinguished from prisons where individuals who are convicted of a crime serve their sentences, jails are mostly detention centers for people who are arrested and charged with a crime but have yet to have their case settled. Jails serve a unique role because they are the entry point into the correctional system and characteristically resemble a revolving door between low–income communities of color and prisons. In 1987, for example, 12.7 million arrests led to 8.7 million jail admissions, yet only 580,000 people were serving sentences in state or federal prisons. The vast majority of people who spend time in jail are released on bail, allowed to plea bargain, or are moved into the parole or probation systems.[16] The fact that a disproportionate number of the women inmates at Rikers are people of color is related to the general rise in crime, more stringent criminal justice policies, diminishing opportunity, and biased practices in the criminal justice system. Some criminologists have even suggested that increasingly the purpose of jails in contemporary society has become to "manage the underclass in American society."[17]

Despite the trend of seemingly mass incarceration, social science research has virtually ignored jails as a research site, even though more than thirty times as many people pass through jails as prisons. Studies of battered women in jail, as a distinct and different population, have been particularly scarce; however, a few recent studies of battered women in prison suggest that significant numbers of battered women are detained in correctional facilities like Rikers Island. Most notable was a survey conducted by the Correctional Association that found that over half of all female inmates were victims of physical abuse, and thirty-five percent had been sexually abused. The statistics corroborate the findings from legislative hearings held at the Bedford Hills Maximum Security Correctional Facility for Women in New York state.[18]

While seemingly unrelated, the intersection of these intellectual, social, and political trends, and, more specifically, my concern for the population of the women whose life experiences led them to this intersection, stimulated my interest and led me to the Rose M. Singer Center at Rikers Island Correctional Facility where, from June 1991 to February 1992, I conducted life–history interviews with women who were detained there. Their lives embodied the clash of these trends; repressive criminal justice policies, scholarship that subsumed or ignored their experiences, and a social–change movement that did not address their unique needs. But their stories told of more than the macroanalytic dimensions of contemporary social life for African American women from low–income communities; they also had a deeply personal dimension. The women's stories told of how the de- velopment of a distinctly female identity in African American families influenced the dynamics of their adult intimate relationships in a way that left them vulnerable to abuse. Their stories ultimately bespoke how violence, the threat of violence, and other forms of coercion by their male partners led them to crime. Out of these stories emerged the gender entrapment model, in which public trends and private events find new meaning and offer insight into a frequently misunderstood population.

2

LIFE HISTORIES

Listening to the Women's Stories

IN THIS CHAPTER, I will review the methodology that informed my approach to the writing of this book. In some ways, the process of conducting interviews and developing a theory is a story in and of itself. Again, it reflects my interest in offering an alternative view of the women's lives in order to shift the dominant social science paradigms and in encouraging a more respectful and humane public–policy response to the problems of crime, violence against women, poverty, racism and gender discrimination. At very least, this chapter will help readers understand the women's stories. For knowing how I came to understand the women I met may help others understand them better too.

The principal research method I used to understand the experiences of the African–American battered women was to analyze the findings from life–history interviews obtained through use of the interview schedule of open–ended questions. I chose the life–history method because it is particularly useful in gathering information about stigmatized, uncomfortable, or difficult circumstances in subjects' lives.[1] Compared to other, more structured qualitative methods, conducting life–history interviews offered a more intense opportunity to learn about subjects' backgrounds, opinions, feelings, and the meanings they give to the mundane events and the exceptional experiences in their lives.[2]

A review of the sociological studies of similar populations that have used the life–history methodology further establishes its advantages. Joyce Ladner's landmark study of the life of Black adolescent girls significantly shifted the sociological understanding of life in the Black community in the late 1970s. Ladner's findings were based on systematic, open–ended life–history interviews about the attitudes and behaviors of thirty women. Her study was concerned with their choices of role models and the influences of values, customs, and traditions of the Black community on their gender identities. Ladner's analysis included a consideration of structural variables such as kin relationships and the women's access to institutional resources. Of particular interest to this study of incarcerated battered women were Ladner's questions about perceived "disparity between the resources she has with which to achieve her goals in life and the stated aspirations." [3] For her research, as for this study, it was important to learn from the women themselves rather than approach the interviews with rigid preconceived notions—especially in terms of normative and deviant behavior. Sandra Harding has credited Ladner's work with providing a "thought–provoking analysis of the relationships between methodological, theoretical, epistemological, political and ethical dimensions of social science research." [4]

Another influential study, conducted by Carol Stack, of urban kinship networks also used an open–ended interview schedule designed to detect and describe the most meaningful elements of daily life for Black women in their communities. In her book *All Our Kin*, she characterizes her interviews as "informal conversations" based on general theoretical issues of interest to her sample, including social and domestic relations, gossip (informal community–building networks), kinship and residence patterns, and child rearing/parenting. Like Ladner's methodology, Stack's approach closely resembled the life–history interview method that was used in this study.

Judith Rollins's book, *Between Women*, documents the relationship between domestics and their employers using a similar interview method. Rollins states that her choice of unstructured, open–ended interviews was based on the premise that the ideas, attitudes, thoughts, and emotions of people must be examined and understood in order to develop policies and programs that re-arrange the exploitative aspects of social relationships. As I was in this study, Rollins was interested in the ways that gender and race influence interpersonal and social relationships, and how access to institutional resources are central issues in women's lives. Rollins's methodology was particularly helpful in captur-ing the complexities that arise in relationships of domination that are influenced by emotional and social bonds, such as mar-riage. Rollins's epistemological approach was based on the as-sumption that the ideas of women who have experienced the phenomenon under study are the most important to understand. She thus entered into the research process with intellectual openness, allowing patterns to emerge during the interviews.[5] While her forty focused interviews followed a guide, Rollins en-couraged the women to elaborate on the aspects of their lives that were most important *to them*, a methodology I followed in this study.

Of those studies of women that used the life–history method, Eleanor Miller's population most closely resembles this study. Her life–history interviews of seventy women who were in-volved in criminal activities yielded detailed accounts of the paths women took from their families of origin to "street life." In her study, Miller was able not only to describe individual cases, but also to document a general pattern that incorporated individual differences, structural influences, and cultural factors that were critical to interpreting the criminality of the women in her sample. By her own account, Miller's life histories "were not complete life histories" but rather were "topical" life histories based on themes gleaned from a review of the literature that was relevant to her study.

While none of these studies focused on the same qualitative population that I interviewed, the methodology they used—in-depth interviews and analysis according to themes from the lit-erature—served to establish the rationale for using the life–his-tory approach in this study. For me, the life–history method was appropriate and effective in discovering the complex interactions of events and the ongoing social process that were associated with the African American battered women's gender–role development, their experience of intimate violence, and the circumstances that led to arrest. The approach allowed for a focus on both a gender–specific analysis to social analysis of the population, *as well as* attention to the nuances that varied across racial/ ethnic or cultural categories, hence illuminating the key elements of the gender–entrapment theoretical model.

The Three Subgroups

I chose to focus on African American battered women incarcerated at Rikers Island Correctional Facility because I believed they were uniquely vulnerable to the trends discussed in Chapter One. Their experiences in the private as well as the public sphere allowed me to explore the relationship between four variables: 1) culturally determined gender roles; 2) prevailing social conditions affecting the African American communities; 3) hierarchical institutional arrangements in contemporary society based on race/ethnicity; and 4) biased practices within the criminal justice system. My understanding of the experiences of the African American battered women on these four variables were compared to two other groups of women detained at Rikers Island: African American women who were *not* battered and *white* women who were. Comparing the life–history interviews of these three groups helped to refine the gender–entrapment theory by isolating the effects of race/ethnicity and violence in an intimate relationship.

The decision to focus on African American battered women intentionally allowed me to focus on their experiences and perceptions, thereby locating them at the center of my analysis. This served to counter the mainstream understanding of women's involvement in crime and to challenge the normative tendency of feminist social science research which typically considers the dominant experience of white women as the basis for comparison. This decision is methodologically consistent with the type of grounded–theory analysis used in this study, permitting me to choose a sample based on my interest in developing theory rather than choosing a more random sample upon which generalizations to the overall population could be made.[7] In the service of generating theory, the two comparison groups were used to stimulate theoretical sensitivity as distinct and different from using a "control group" for comparison in other types of re-

The Demographic Profile of the Sample

	African American		White
	Battered	*Non-battered*	*Battered*
N	26	5	6
HOUSEHOLD OF ORIGIN			
Socioeconomic Status			
poor/public assistance	18	4	3
working poor/working class	8	1	3
Composition of Household			
adult woman and man	10	2	4
woman only	11	1	1
more than one woman	4	2	0
institutional setting	1	0	1
Number of Siblings			
0	4	0	0
1–3	15	4	4
4–6	4	0	2
>7	3	1	1
Subjects' Level of Education			
7–11 grade	10	4	3
graduated high school	3	1	2
earned GED	9	0	0
1–3 years college	4	0	1
Observed mother abused	14	1	4
Battered as Adults			
physical abuse	26	NA	6
sexual abuse also	20	NA	5
Use of Services			
police/victims services	3	NA	5
health care providers	7	NA	5
battered women's program	1	NA	4
extended family/friends	5	NA	6
other services (drug programs, counseling, religious organizations)	1	NA	6

(Demographic Profile, continued)

	African American		White
	Battered	*Non–battered*	*Battered*
ILLEGAL ACTIVITY			
Number of Past Incarcerations			
0	15	0	4
1	3	2	0
2–4	6	0	2
>5	2	3	0
Paths to Illegal Activity			
Path 1/ Child Murder	4	0	0
Path 2/ Assaulted other Men	4	0	0
Path 3/ Illegal Sexual Acts	6	0	3
Path 4/ Crime During Assault	3	0	2
Path 5/ Economic Crime	5	1	0
Path 6/ Illegal Drug Activity	4	4	1

search.[8] While the original sample still did not reflect the universe of experiences, by including racial/ethnic and experiential variations a more complex and textured analysis could be conducted. The interviews with the African American non–battered women and the white battered women helped focus on a gender–specific analysis that attended to the nuances that varied across racial/ethnic or cultural categories. Hence, rather than including their experiences in the analysis, per se, the comparison groups served to illuminate the key elements of the gender–entrapment theoretical model.

OPERATIONAL DEFINITION
OF INTIMATE VIOLENCE

The identification of women to be interviewed and the methodology selected to discuss the effects of gender entrapment was dependent upon the operational definition of the concept of intimate violence. The authors of the CTS scale define violence as "an act carried out with the intention or perceived intention of causing physical pain or injury to another person,"[9] a definition that concurs with those of other experts in the field. The concept of "assault" that is often used in the legal literature, taken from the FBI's *Uniform Crime Reports*, suggests "unlawful intention of inflicting or attempted, threatened inflicting of injury upon another person."[10] Here it is important to note that the current legal scholarship on domestic violence has amended the definition from an injury–based concept to include psychological abuse. According to the *Encyclopedia of Crime and Justice* and also the *Uniform Crime Reports*, "attempts and threats are included in the tabulation of aggravated assault, it is not necessarily that an injury result."[11] Some social scientists who study intimate violence make the distinction between "instrumental" and "expressive" violence. Instrumental violence connotes abusive or threatening activities that are a means to an end, whereas expressive violence serves as an end unto itself. It is generally agreed in the literature that most male–to–female violence in intimate relationships is characteristically not expressive abuse, but is typically instrumental in nature.[12]

While there is considerable ambiguity in the legal and social science conceptualization and, therefore, the *measurement* of the concepts, these definitions informed the operational definition of intimate violence used in this study. As previously discussed, efforts are underway to attempt to remedy this problem. For the purposes of this study, I defined intimate violence as the intentional, willful infliction of physical assaults, threats of assaults, emotional abuse, or coercion by one partner in an intimate relationship towards the other.[13]

HOW THE SAMPLE WAS SELECTED

Based on this definition of intimate violence, the selection of the sample of women to be interviewed for this study was purposeful and deliberate. The practice of "theoretical sampling" was used to select other women to interview. This decision was methodologically consistent with grounded–theory analysis, permitting me to choose a sample based on my interest in developing theory rather than choosing a more random sample upon which generalizations to the overall population could be made.[14] Any African American woman who was an inmate detained at the Rose M.

Singer Center at Rikers Island was eligible to be interviewed if she:

1. identified herself as a battered woman or had a history of violence in her intimate adult relationship(s) or had been physically and/or emotionally abused by a husband, boyfriend, or live-in partner;

2. responded affirmatively to twelve out of the nineteen items on the Conflict Tactics Scale;

3. was psychologically fit for interview and not in need of acute medical or psychological intervention, as determined by the Montefiore/Rikers Island Prison Health Service; and

4. signed the informed-consent form.

RECRUITING AND SCREENING

The women whose stories are told in this book were recruited from four sources, all of which emphasized the voluntary and anonymous nature of the study. First, those respondents in a study being conducted during the same time frame titled "Risk Factors for Sexually Transmitted Disease, Cervical Dysplasia and Tuberculosis in Incarcerated Women" who identified themselves as battered women were asked to volunteer for this study. Second, the Montefiore Mental Health Service and Department of Corrections Social Service staff were asked to publicize the study among their clients who might fit the criteria. Third, the Inmates' Council was contacted to assist in volunteer recruitment. Fourth, women who attended the weekly Domestic Violence Support Group sponsored by the Department of Corrections were also asked if they were willing to volunteer for the study. Informed consent was obtained from each woman prior to the life-history interview. Because of the complex nature of consent in such a setting, I carefully explained to each woman who volunteered the purpose of the study, the implications of signing the form, and the process that ensured anonymity.

The enrollment process for volunteers included a brief screening interview at which time the CTS was administered. Real names, aliases, and the women's book and case identification numbers were kept in a log book and used only to locate those who had been referred to the study. A study number was assigned to each set of field notes, which were stored off-site in a

secure file to which only I had access. The list of women interviewed for this book was destroyed once the data from each interview had been coded, thus ensuring the complete anonymity
of the respondents.

As described below, the results of the life–history interviews
were coded according to themes that emerged from the review of
the literature, and analyzed in aggregate form. In discussing the
study and recounting the life stories in the following chapters of
this book, where any individual case is cited, a pseudonym is
used and identifying characteristics have been disguised or omit-
ted to protect the women's anonymity.

HOW DATA WERE COLLECTED

Data were collected using an interview schedule I designed. It
guided, rather than defined, the life–history interviews that were
conducted with thirty–seven women over a nine–month period
in a private space in the health clinic or one of the housing areas
in the Rose M. Singer Center at Rikers Island Correctional Facility. Each interview lasted approximately three hours. In keeping
with the type of qualitative research that the life–history method
represents, the specific content of the interview was determined,
to a great extent, by the responses from each woman I interviewed. At a minimum, I asked each woman to describe her family background and home environment, the history, nature, and
extent of violence in her intimate relationship(s), and, to a lesser
extent, her involvement in the criminal justice system. Together each woman and I reflected on and interpreted her experience. I was interested in each woman's *own* version of her experiences.

Data collection involved more than conducting the life–history interviews. Prior to developing the interview schedule, I
spent five months at the Rose M. Singer Center, meeting with
women inmates in focus groups, talking with them informally,
observing the daily operations of the facility, and attending a series
of conferences sponsored by the Rikers Island Women's Committee,
where women detained in the facility presented testimony about
the conditions of their lives before and after coming to Rikers
Island. Additionally, I served as a consultant on another study
where I interviewed women as they entered the jail.

The combination of these experiences in the setting prior to initiating the research for this study afforded me an opportunity to become familiar with the everyday lives of the women detained there and to hear, from their perspectives, what their overall experiences had been. I recorded in a field journal my observations, key terms and phrases, the names of individuals who might facilitate my access in the jail, and my general reactions to the setting and the interview. This process was extremely valuable to the data collection. My interview schedule and the research design were thus informed by firsthand knowledge of the population and the setting, as well as my past experience in the field and my subsequent interpretation of the broader social context of the study. By the time I conducted the interviews, I had some knowledge of the women's lives and of the pace of life at the jail. I knew something of the meaning the women gave to external and internal events, the troubled places in which the women had found themselves, and the conditions of their lives. While writing this book, I have continued to spend time with women detained at Rikers Island.

The data collection was affected by a number of institutional factors that shaped the research design and process, as described in Chapter One. Most notable was the fact that the Rose M. Singer Center is a temporary detaining institution where inmates' legal status is in the process of being determined. The women I interviewed never knew when they would be summoned to court or whether or when they would be released, transferred to another institution, convicted of a crime, or sentenced to become a ward of the New York state prison system. This created a series of subjective experiences for me as a researcher that affected data collection.

First, the nature of the questions and the length of time that we spent talking created a certain intensity in my relationship with the women I got to know during the interviews. We talked for a long time about topics that many had never talked about in such detail. Most of the women expressed an appreciation for the opportunity to speak freely, for the attention and the flexible, non–judgmental approach I used in the interviews. Their appreciation was an important incentive for me to endure the sometimes difficult obstacles to conducting the interviews as well as the tedious and troubling content. On some days I would wait three or four hours for an officer to release a woman to the area in which I was scheduled to interview her. Other times, I would travel to Rikers Island only to be denied access because there was an "alarm." Usually I could locate women only a few times after I interviewed them to follow up, as most were transferred, sentenced, or "lost" in the system within a few days. Mostly, I was affected by my own frustration and anger as I observed how the women were treated and learned of the legal and bureaucratic barriers to the expeditious resolution of their cases.

Because I assumed multiple roles in the institution (field worker, consultant, outside service provider), my work sometimes included facilitating access to health, legal, and social services at the Rose M. Singer Center for women who were in need. I also had relationships with several outside programs, and at times I made referrals for women to be seen by an agency once they were released from the jail. Similarly, I had visited several women's prisons in New York state, and I could make referrals to programs for those women who might be sentenced and transferred there.

In several instances I felt an ethical conflict between my role as a researcher and as an advocate. Many times, it was difficult for me to remain detached, and I found it impossible to avoid becoming invested in the outcome of the women's cases. At times, I failed to conceal my own emotional responses to their life stories. It helped that, for the most part, I was able to distinguish myself from the women because the events of my life story, so far, had been significantly different from theirs. However, at moments I felt the distance between us narrowing. I have encountered two of the women I interviewed on the street in the community in which I live; another has a sister who is a member of an organization with which I am affiliated; and several have written me letters, finding my address on various institutional mailing lists.

My closeness to the inmates became personally problematic on several occasions. During the data-collection phase of the research, I was mistaken for an inmate three times by correctional officers. When a prosecutor learned about my study, she threatened to subpoena my field notes to use against a woman whom I had interviewed. Fortunately, this threat was never realized. However, it illustrates how the nature of the data–collection process that enabled me to use myself and my experiences to be close to the women I interviewed also posed a series of dilemmas for my role as a researcher. Overall, it did not interfere with my ability to effectively focus the interviews on the research questions designed for this study. On the contrary, my physical and emotional closeness enhanced my data–collection ability and experience; for I knew at some level that I, too, have faced difficult choices, and that, but for my privilege, I also would have had more limited options.

THE ANALYSIS OF THE LIFE–HISTORY INTERVIEWS

This was a descriptive study designed to develop an alternative model of explaining women's illegal activities. The analysis of data from this type of non–experimental, qualitative study seeks first and foremost to capture the women's own feelings and views and the meanings they give to the events in their lives. The specific process of data analysis used in this study was based on the grounded–theory approach to qualitative research. Developed by Barney Glasser and Ansel Strauss in the early 1960s, grounded theory is influenced by the tradition of the Chicago School of Sociology that utilized field observations and intensive interviews as data–collection techniques in order to grasp and emphasize the social actor's point of view of social reality and social change.[15] According to Strauss, "the goal of grounded theory is to generate a theory that accounts for a pattern of behavior that is relevant and problematic for those involved."[16] The grounded–theory method of data analysis was, therefore, particularly well suited for developing the theory of gender entrapment.

The data analysis was undertaken simultaneously with the data collection. After each interview was conducted, I transcribed my field notes and reviewed them to identify the key elements: the critical events, the women's emotional responses, factors that influenced their behaviors, and the conditions in their households and communities as the women described them. This process of reviewing the research questions and studying the field notes led to the initial coding schema.

As the coding of the interviews progressed, common themes began to emerge, which allowed for constant comparisons. Gradually, broader categories emerged, and I was able to look at the relationship between three core categories: gender–identity development, violence in intimate relationships, and participation in illegal activities. The organization of these relationships served as the theoretical underpinnings of the gender–entrapment model.

The analysis continued until the data was "saturated," meaning that the findings from the life–history interviews no longer contributed new information about the three categories or properties of the categories under study.[17] Two months into the analysis of the data, several techniques commonly utilized by qualitative researchers were added to the process of developing the gender–entrapment theoretical model. First, I drew a diagram to provide a visual image of the integration of gender–identity development, violence in intimate relationships, and the women's involvement in illegal activities. Later, I wrote theoretical memos as a way to keep track of the coding results, to stimulate hypotheses, and to reinforce the generation of the theory of gender entrapment, and to share the findings with the women I interviewed.

The final stage of data analysis and theory development was to consider the findings within the broader sociological context. This process involved conceptualizing the sequence of events that generally constituted the women's life patterns in order to systematically sort the themes into categories that illuminated the social processes of gender entrapment.[18] While the contextualized life–history interviews were intended to illustrate some of the social processes that had influenced this particular group of women, the analysis and documentation of the life histories that begin in Chapter Three stress each woman's own version of her experiences.[19]

THE LIMITATIONS OF THIS STUDY

While the strength of qualitative research is that it provided in–depth information about the interactive variables of the lives of the women I talked with, conspicuous weaknesses are inherent in the method. The particular limitations of the life–history method used in this study fall into three categories: 1) ethical and logistical dilemmas; 2) the validity of the information presented; and 3) the generalizability of the research findings.

As previously mentioned, the jail setting itself posed significant obstacles to conducting any type of research, especially in–depth interviews that are sensitive in nature. My ability to locate, interview, and follow up any particular woman I talked with was limited by the lack of privacy, the restrictions on movement of civilians and inmates alike, and distractions such as unexpected family visits, court appearances, and spontaneous releases. Additionally, since most of the women whose stories are told in this book were *charged* but not yet convicted of the crimes for which they were arrested, their legal situations were precarious, and the potential harm of disclosing information was significant. Many of the women were arrested for serious and sensitive crimes, such as felonious possession of an illegal sub-stance or child endangerment. Because of their pending legal cases, most of the women interviewed for this book were uni-quely vulnerable, and some of the women may have felt com-pelled to withhold or distort information that they felt might discredit their legal cases or affect their treatment in jail.

A second limitation of the study was related to the overall question of validity that surrounds qualitative research. Most self–reporting methods of data collection in social science re-search raise questions about validity and reliability of findings. Especially on sensitive topics such as violence, intimate rela-tionships, and criminal behavior, these considerations loom be-fore any researcher and her audience. At best, all self–reports are subject to memory errors and unconscious distortions of what is reported.[20] However, it has been generally accepted that because of the shame associated with being a battered woman, distor-tions that *minimize* the violence are more common than those that *exaggerate* the extent of violence in intimate relationships.[21]

A third limitation of the methodological approach used in this study is the extent to which its findings can be generalized. As previously noted, the literature on qualitative analysis suggests that while life–history interviews provide in–depth information about those women who are interviewed, the tendency to "miss the forest for the trees" is notable. In the analysis phase of the project, I had to avoid perceiving an explicit or implied pattern in the overall population when, in fact, the findings may represent only the particular women who were interviewed for this book. Just as generalizability is compromised by the subjective nature of the life–history methodology, the ability to replicate the study may also be limited by the unstructured nature of the interview schedule.

The final limitation is related to the use of a model group and smaller comparison groups. While this approach is consistent with the methodology selected for this study, it should not be construed to conclude that African American battered women are more negatively affected by the circumstances in their households of origin, their racial/ethnic identities, violence against women, or the pull toward illegal activities. It is therefore important to emphasize that the analytical approach used in this study *intentionally* privileged the experience of African American battered women, and less so the African American women who were not battered and the white battered women, in order to develop the theory of gender entrapment.

These limitations, while no doubt significant, are balanced by the rich multitextured data that emerged from the life–history interviews. More importantly, it served the overall purpose of the study, which was to explore and explain a *particular* set of women's experiences well so that broad social trends of exclusion, marginalization, and criminalization of African American battered women from low–income communities are reversed.

3

GENDER-IDENTITY DEVELOPMENT

"Growing up as a Black girl was hard, but good."

AS ONE of the principal organizing units of society, the family or household serves several functions: to socialize its members, to provide a vehicle for meeting basic material and emotional needs, and to transmit social norms and values. It is also considered a key determinant in the development of individual identity and the subsequent behavior of social actors. Cultural forces influence household units by interjecting ideology, thereby providing, as Leith Mullings puts it, a "frame of reference through which people attempt to deal with the circumstances in which they find themselves."[1]

From a broader sociological perspective, the organization of households and the ordering of their members by gender and generation serve as a mechanism of social control, enforcing a division of labor that shapes public as well as domestic relationships. As such, the ideological, cultural, and social construction of the household establishes a foundation for the reproduction of hegemonic roles with regard to gender and generation. Even those social actors whose experiences fall outside of the dominant family form because of historical circumstances, cultural beliefs, race/ethnicity, or class are influenced by family ideology and the organization of society around a generalized (albeit rarely practiced) notion of the family.

Findings from the life–history interviews conducted with the African American battered women whose stories are told in this book showed that the women had been significantly influenced by the structure and function of their households, their cultural frames of reference, the gendered and generational division of labor, and the positions of their families in the dominant social order. Beginning with a discussion of the women's positions in their households of origin, this chapter will trace their gender–identity development by describing their images of and relationships with adults in their households, including the extent to which the women experienced or observed abuse. A distinct pattern emerges among those factors that influenced the women's vulnerability, risk–taking behaviors, their role models, and the gender differences between male and female childhood roles in their households of origin. The chapter concludes with a discussion of the relationship between racial/ethnic identity and family loyalty, which, when taken with the other factors, created the particular dynamic of gender entrapment for the African American battered women in this study.

These findings, as discussed in this chapter, show how the African American battered women's vulnerability to gender entrapment began as their gender identity was constructed in their households of origin, and was later influenced by the social positions of their African American families in the public sphere. I will show how these influences led to the creation of intimate relationships that left these women particularly vulnerable to abuse, which, in turn, set them on unique paths to illegal activities and incarceration at Rikers Island Correctional Facility.

THEIR PLACE IN THEIR HOUSEHOLD

When they compared themselves to other children in their households, the women I interviewed for this book held one of three distinct positions that were associated with the three subgroups in the overall sample population. The first group of women received extra privileges, attention, and resources, indicating the families' emotional and material investment in these particular children to meet high standards of success. The second group of responses consisted of women who felt they had been average children. They considered themselves of equal value or importance to other members of their households. The third group of women I interviewed had relatively low status when compared to other children, being routinely assigned extraordinary responsibilities for household maintenance and receiving significantly less interest and resources from the adult members of their households.

Findings from interviews with African American battered women indicated that almost all of them held privileged positions in their families of origin. Describing the benefits of their privileged status over other children in very concrete ways, they reported having more clothing and other possessions, a disproportionate amount of discretionary spending money given the relatively low household income, and more frequent inclusion in social activities and cultural events outside the home.

As Sebina, a thirty–two–year–old African American battered woman detained on a charge of co–conspiracy to murder said:

> I grew up as the favorite girl in a close–knit, conservative family. We were poor, but I had it all: dancing lessons at the YMCA, ice skating in Central Park, library books, toys, and lots of other stuff. Real feminine. I went to Catholic school on a scholarship and was the nuns' best student. I was my church debutante, a perfect Girl Scout. I believed that I was really their special something, and my folks went out of their way to prove how special I was—every day in a different way.

Similarly, April, a thirty–year–old African American battered woman in jail awaiting trial on an arson charge, said:

> All the adults in my family worked hard to meet the needs of the children. My mother was a day worker during the day, and a cook in a local restaurant at nights and weekends. My father was a custodian during the day and worked as the superintendent of our apartment building. I didn't want for anything. My parents gave me all of the money I wanted, while at the same time showing me how important working hard was. Everything I had was better than what my siblings or friends had, and since I always shared with them, I always had lots of friends. I guess you could say that from my earliest days I had lots of people interested in me.

Lynne's experience also fit this pattern. She was a twenty-eight-year-old African American detainee facing a mandatory sentence of two to four years if found guilty on a felonious drug charge. She said:

> I was raised in a house with my mother, a brother, and a sister. I was the favorite, the youngest, the one who was my family's pride and joy. I was only smarter because they thought I *should* be, and I had the most energy. Actually, my mother identified with me because I pushed her to have fun, to be alive rather than just working all of the time. I was always looking for a man to take care of her. I was always playing jokes on my family, and I brought more spirit to the house. I was rewarded with the gifts of more food, money, clothes, and chances to be "in the world."

For most of the women in this group, the privileged position in their households included an affective component as well as a material one: their elevated status had an emotional or expressive quality. The women in this group recalled the adults in their households or extended families verbalizing appreciation for their personal qualities, articulating hopes for their futures, and using them as positive examples for other children.

Letisha, a thirty-seven-year-old African American battered woman detained on a forgery charge, reported:

> I grew up in a household with my mother, father, five brothers and four sisters. It was the second marriage for both my folks. They each brought children to the household, but I am the only child born of the union between them....I am the only *real* daughter they have. They loved each other so much that I got pulled into my mom and dad's close circle of loving, while the other children did not. They really treated me like a princess. I got lots of extra attention and encouragement, because they put all of their stock in me as a girl because they felt that I had a better chance of making it than the boys. My mother worked for the government, and my father worked on and off as a night worker at a newspaper. When they were gone, I got to be in charge. When they were home, I was the one they doted on. I really think they liked, loved, and believed in me best.

Their privileged status in their households created a dialectic for this subgroup that ultimately became a critical element in their gender entrapment. While they developed a sense of themselves as "unique" or "extraordinary," being "special" brought with it a feeling of being "different." In retrospect, the subgroup of African American battered women expressed ambivalence about their childhood positions, recalling how with the privileged status came responsibilities for caring for younger siblings, pressure to do extraordinarily well in school, and the burden of being their caretakers' confidantes. In addition to the concrete and emotional benefits of their elevated positions in their households, these women reported having felt burdened by the pressure to meet the expectations that would *maintain* their privileged status. Some described how the fear of losing their privileges propelled them into constant attempts to further heighten their status in their households.

Letisha continued:

> I remember not knowing what was harder, being perfect or trying to stay perfect. I got all of the extras in my household. Sometimes I tried to reject all of the attention or share it with my brothers and sisters. It made me feel too different from them when actually I wanted to be around the other kids, *not* separate from them. My parents counted on me to be perfect, and it really cut down on my fun. Actually it was a lot of work to be the favorite. And in the end, look at where I am now.

The sense that Letisha and other women in this subgroup got about the conditional nature of the love, affection, respect, and the need to constantly work to maintain their status in relationships was a recurring theme from early childhood. This dynamic had a particularly gendered aspect. As young girls, the African American women who were battered saw themselves as critical family members, upon whom many people depended. They felt that their roles were distinctly different from those of the male children in their families. They had high self–esteem and felt very powerful, and yet their identities were wrapped up in pleasing others and accommodating the needs of others. The women described feeling a sense of responsibility to "make good" on themselves for their families' emotional and, to a lesser extent, material investments in their futures, even when their social options for education, work, and a traditional family life were limited. The dialectic of being relatively privileged and feeling burdened by that status is an essential element of their gender entrapment.

In contrast, the pattern that emerged among the five African American women who were not battered was distinctly different. These women described feeling more like "average children," with similar status to the other members of their household; they were not favored by extra privileges, possessions, or attention. As the following cases illustrate, the African American women who were not battered felt they were generally treated fairly, not specially, relative to other female children in their families or extended households.

Karen, a twenty–year–old African American woman who was pregnant with her fourth child, was detained in the prenatal dormitory at Rikers Island on charges of prostitution. She grew up with her mother, father, and three siblings in a small apartment in public housing. Her mother worked at a fast–food restaurant. Her father worked sporadically as a gardener. Financially, they were comfortable, typically sharing resources with other units of the extended family. Karen said:

> My parents were not so into us. My brothers were into themselves, and I was pretty much alone. I grew up in the middle of things, without any company. They were truly overprotective of me. I mean it's not like they really *cared* about me. They said they kept me inside so that I wouldn't get hurt, but I think it was so that no one had to be bothered watching me. I stayed in the house most of the time, and so I would cook, and I had to clean up for the whole family. When my niece came to live with us, it got better because no one cared too much for her either. At least we shared the work between us. I'd say it wasn't good for me in my family, but I guess it wasn't bad either.

The findings revealed a difference between the households of the African American women who were not battered and the households of other children in their neighborhoods. The women's descriptions of the differences suggested that their families were more economically and socially marginalized than others in their communities. Yet, without the expectation, the position, or the means, they did not feel the pressure to maintain status, and they did not try to affect the nature of their households by their behavior. As such, they typically described more carefree, less burdened childhood experiences than the African American battered women for whom privileges became vulnerabilities.

Anita, age thirty–five, detained on a drug charge, grew up in a large, lively, warm household occupied by lots of young people who assumed caretaking roles for each other because the adults were usually absent. She recalled:

> Sometimes our folks just left because there were just too many of us... they were outnumbered. Money–wise we were a very poor house, living in too small a space, living off other families and friends, usually without enough food or clothes, certainly no extras. Getting an education, hard work, and religion were given lip service, but none of the children in my family graduated from high school and no one made any money to give anyone else. We were the neighborhood charity case... but it wasn't too bad on most days. At least there were lots of people around to hang out with. It was kind of fun, no pressure, no pleasure, and no pain—just getting through the day in a real kidlike way.

In sum, the five African American women who were not battered were economically and socially disadvantaged compared to the battered African American women. They were more likely to have low or no stable income, to have been raised in larger households, and to be less attended to by the adults in their lives. They were left to themselves, highly influenced by peers rather than adults, and did not expect to accomplish the dominant society's measure of success.

The findings from the life–history interviews of the six white women who were battered also revealed a different pattern from that of the battered African American women. They too were not materially or emotionally privileged, but in comparison to the African American women who were not battered, they were even worse off when growing up. They generally felt deprived, undervalued, and, in some cases, scapegoated when compared to other children in their households. They described ways that their caretakers habitually slighted them in terms of material resources, attention, and, most importantly from their perspective, affection. The women experienced this relative deprivation most acutely in comparison to their brothers. Childhood for these women was characterized by weighty responsibilities for ongoing household duties without reward, recognition, or privilege.

In contrast to the African American battered women, the white battered women grew up expecting lower status in intimate relationships and were, therefore, less vulnerable to gender entrapment. As Shirley said:

> Basically, I didn't really have any kind of childhood. I had to do everything from taking care of the house to taking care of my sister and brother. It was more than regular household chores.... Like I mean from the time I was seven I cooked dinner every night, which was hard since we hardly had enough food, and I washed the clothes so we could go to school. I was the one who woke everyone up, who put everyone to sleep and who tried as best I could to keep everyone as happy as possible. I felt like I was having to take care of everything, like it was expected of me and that I couldn't stop and just be a little girl.

As is true for many low–income families, all of the women in this study described working hard as young children in their households, symbolizing for some a strong family work ethic that was gender–specific. For others, working hard was related to the families' significant need for the female children's ongoing contributions to the functioning of the households. In those instances where the male children contributed at all, it was generally during adolescence through wage–producing activities outside the home. Not surprisingly, the women reported that the boys' involvement in the labor force brought high esteem for their brothers. This pattern was more common in the white families than in either of the subgroups of African American women.

To fully understand the gender–entrapment theoretical model, it is important to distinguish between the three subgroups in this study on the *meaning* of childhood work in their households. The African American battered women initiated household tasks, felt appreciated and rewarded for their work, and believed that their heightened status was reinforced when they assumed family responsibilities. Their work included emotional work—providing support, encouragement, and comfort to other children as well as to the adults in their households. Again, this pattern repeated in their abusive adult relationships.

For the other two groups, household work was obligatory, and tasks were assigned to them as punishment. These women recalled that their efforts brought them negative or critical attention rather than reward, a sense of accomplishment, or privileged status. When they compared themselves to other children in their families or neighborhoods, the white battered women, in particular, felt as if they had a disproportionately high amount of responsibility that resulted in an unhappy, stressful childhood that they described as void of peer relationships, pleasure, and interest from adults.

It is important to emphasize that the amount of material and emotional privilege and the degree to which the children were required to work in their households of origin did *not* vary by structural factors such as household income or number of siblings, as might be expected. Rather, the concept of position within the household was relative to the other children in *the same* household. The significant finding was that the African American battered women were more likely to be favorite children (especially as girls), and the comparison groups of African American non–battered women and white women were either average or had lower status than their siblings. This distinction illustrates one of the ironic aspects of gender entrapment: the African American battered women's identities as competent, resourceful, potential–filled girl children, which was constructed and reinforced early in their family relationships and household arrangements, ultimately left them exposed and more vulnerable to harsh reality than the other women in this sample.

FEMALE CARETAKERS AND MALE INFLUENCES

A second pattern of responses to the life–history interviews that varied by subgroup in this study was the women's image of and relationship with their female caretakers, and the influence that adult men had on their childhood experiences. In all of the cases in this study, the women's primary caretakers were women or groups of women. In sixteen of the thirty–seven cases, the women I interviewed were raised in households where both parents lived, with the male partner assuming the role of secondary caretaker, in the model of "traditional fatherhood." Whether an adult man was present or absent was a significant factor in shaping the women's identities and future experiences, and varied by subgroup in this study.

In retrospect, the African American battered women, as children, had an idealized notion of who their mothers or adult women caretakers were. They recalled having deep respect for the women's personal attributes. They admired the people their mothers were, and, even as children, they had a keen sense of the sacrifices the older women made for their families. The women characteristically used terms to describe their mothers or female caretakers that demonstrated reverence: "perseverance," "disciplined," "strong sense of morality."

As Crystal, a twenty–seven–year–old African American battered woman, arrested for arson, said:

> My relationship with my mother was never very close, although I always knew she was in my corner. She worked for some wealthy white people, and that took a lot of her energy away for me. She stayed with them during the week. I couldn't believe that she was so generous about that. She never missed a day of work. They disrespected her, but she never complained. She was like the perfect, loyal, hardworking maid. And on weekends she was the servant of the Lord; spending all weekend involved with the church. I know she must have been tired, but she never let on. To me she was a wise woman who everyone could depend on.

However, when these women described the relationships they had with their female caretakers, they described conflicting feelings and experiences. Crystal continued:

> Even though everyone depended on my mother, none of us were able to be really close to her. She was kind of distant, like she really lived in her own world; working and praying as hard as she did, she didn't let herself be open to anyone else. Whenever I tried to talk with her, she was distracted by something else. She influenced me a lot, but it wasn't because she was around me very much. I resented her perfection and the lack of mothering she gave me. It was hard to live with her moralistic judgment staring me in the face all the time.

The collective sense gleaned from the life–history interviews was that most of these women described periods of distance and tension with their mothers that resulted in painful memories of episodic interruptions in their contact with their families. Selma, age thirty, detained on a murder charge, said:

> In my family, everything was very organized. Everyone knew the rules. We did what was needed to be done. I did better in

school than anyone else. My parents were stable and reliable employees, and I became the most stable and reliable child. Most of all, our family believed that we should stay in good standing with each other; it was a moral obligation I in particular had. But I started to feel rebellious, wanting more passion and emotion, not just talk but *real* love. I got pregnant in eleventh grade by my first boyfriend, who was totally irresponsible, but he treated me like precious candy. Now *that* sure got my family's emotion going.... They didn't talk to me, their "favorite child," for *six* months!

The women's images of and relationships with their fathers or adult male household members were distinctly different from their images of and relationships with the adult women in their lives. The findings indicated less reverent feelings, less idolizing, and more affection toward the men than the women in their households. The women described interactions with their fathers or father figures as having a more "peerlike" than parental quality. For some, the impressions of adult men contained references to the women's feeling superior to them. Even as children, some women recalled feeling sorry for their fathers' inabilities to assume more socially acceptable roles.

Janet, age thirty–six, arrested on a murder charge, said:

I grew up with my mom, dad, and four other kids. My dad actually lived across the street, and I moved back and forth between the two households. I was his favorite, which was hard for my mom, because I was her favorite too. While my folks were still all involved in each other's lives, they really didn't get along so well. Daddy continued to support the household so Mama didn't have to work. We were comfortable. We had a car and a nice apartment, especially for the projects. I was born with polio, which meant I had to spend a year in an iron lung. My mom almost died when I was born. She was real sick, too. My dad took care of me during that first year. He did everything—as if he was my mother. It must have been a hard time, because there are no baby pictures of me.... It was as if I was never born. When my dad passed, I was twenty–three and part of me died with him. Part of my heart is gone forever, because the best thing that ever happened to me was that I was my dad's daughter. He really let me in on his life. Like when he admitted to me that he couldn't

read, I taught him how. I was his teacher and his helper. It was
sad for him to have to depend on his kid for things like dealing
with the landlord, but he taught me about the good life in return. He was a gangster, and I only learned after he died that he
made his money as a big–time drug dealer. It's too bad that this
was the only way that he could make it, and I felt sorry for him.
It hurt me to not know the truth because he must have been too
ashamed to talk about it with me. Now look at me, an addict.
Still, to me, my dad was the kindest, best friend I'll ever have.

In these families, the perception was that men were disproportionately harmed by racial inequality and discrimination, which,
for the women I interviewed, explained their fathers' inabilities
to provide economic or social support for their families.

Melanie, age twenty–seven, arrested on a murder charge, said:

We grew up knowing that the Black man had a hard way to go,
and so we didn't expect much from them. My dad was just gone,
like he couldn't face not being a real man in our household. It's
not like we were mad at him, but we felt sorry for him. You
should have heard the sad stories about what used to happen to
him. Once he was even accused of jumping a cop who didn't even
live in the same city. It was awful. Black men—they just have it
hard, and we knew it. He just couldn't do any better by us.

In sum, the twenty–six African American battered women
grew up believing that the women and girls in their households
were in better positions than the men. They recalled thinking
that women were able to get jobs more easily than men, or at
least could apply for public assistance to support their families.
They witnessed the emotional benefits of women's friendships
and experienced the advantages of resource–sharing and concrete
support that characterized relationships among the adult women
they knew.

Here again, the irony of privileged status emerged as a contradiction, setting in motion an interpretive and experiential process that left them vulnerable. For example, having the "privilege" of receiving public assistance included a series of degrading experiences with bureaucracy, just as having the ability
to secure employment meant the "privilege" of working two and
sometimes three jobs. Furthermore, the sense of being privileged

brought with it the responsibility of caring for those who weren't (e.g., men, older family members, and other children), usually with inadequate resources. This dialectical meaning of "privileged status" and "being advantaged," and the organization of private relationships in response to African American men's marginalization in the public sphere, is a fundamental underpinning of the gender–entrapment theoretical model.

The African American women who were not battered recalled their mothers less idealistically. Their descriptions were less glorified, and they did not describe feeling in awe of their mothers' personal qualities. They expressed a more accurate and specific awareness of and sensitivity to the social circumstances that typically limited their mothers' lives.

Toni, age thirty–three, detained for violation of parole on a drug conviction, said:

> We were just a regular family of poor Black folks trying to survive. I was raised with my aunt, my four siblings, and two cousins. My mom tried to hang in there with us, but she just drank too much for her own good. Sometimes I was mad at her, especially when she would be gone for a long time; then I would forgive her and try to understand how hard her life had been. At least she did right by us by hooking us up with my aunt who really took good care of us. My mother worked hard to send money back to the house even when she wasn't there. I think that was pretty good of her. I learned to adjust quickly to the circumstances in our household, which changed a lot. I think she taught me to take care of business.

These women not only understood their mothers' plights, but they identified more with them. They typically remembered growing up believing that they would face obstacles that were similar to those their mothers had faced, and that they would probably respond to problems in similar ways. The women in this group discussed their mothers in terms that recognized both their strengths and their character flaws. Their life stories did not indicate as many periods of tension with their female caretakers as the African American battered women's did.

The fathers of the African American non–battered women were typically physically or emotionally absent during most of their childhood, and the women did not recall close or signifi-

cant relationships with them. This led to feelings of resentment
for some. When compared to the African American battered
women, these women tended to incorporate their mothers' disdain rather than tolerance for their fathers' irresponsibilities, and
at a very early age they generalized it to include the notion that,
categorically, men were not trustworthy.

Toni continued:

> In some ways we were real old–fashioned Black folks. The wom-
> en in my house always took care of business because men just
> weren't any use to us. Like my mother at least kept trying to
> work and take care of us while my father was running away. He
> only came when he wanted something and when we wouldn't
> give it to him.... whatever it was, he would try to take it. I
> think he used to take sex from my mother like that, and if she
> wasn't around, he'd take it from my aunt. I hated him for that.
> We'd lock the house when we saw him coming. When I got older,
> I used to do that to my boyfriends too. None of them are any
> good.

For other African American women who were not battered, it
was as if the male adults in their families were almost irrelevant
to daily life in their households. Men did not occupy a significant emotional, practical, or symbolic place in their early or later
lives. The absence of men was accepted with indifference. As
such, the African American women who were not battered were
less concerned about men's lack of social options and less invested in taking care of them in the domestic sphere than were
the battered African American women.

Contrary to either group of African American women, the
white battered women in this study described families that were
ideologically, and in practice, hierarchical according to generation and gender. There was very little breach of the "adult–
child" distance traditionally associated with the dominant family form. Because activities were highly segregated by gender and
generation, these women generally did not describe intimate relationships with adults of either gender. While their mothers
were typically the primary caretakers for material needs, they
were not described as nurturers of the children's emotional development, but rather as distant or preoccupied. The white wom-
en did not recall confiding in adults or understanding adult life

circumstances, and they tended to avoid contact with the adults. In particular, the women in this subgroup feared their fathers.

Gwen, age thirty–three, detained on a charge of sexual abuse of a minor and sodomy, said:

> I wasn't very loved while I was growing up. I was alone, never included by my brother and sisters, and, as the oldest, I had to do all of the housework. I cooked for the family, washed and ironed our clothes, and cleaned the house. As I got older, I got even more work to do, especially when my mother's health got bad. The other kids were yelled at a lot to work hard, but they knew they didn't really have to listen. They would disobey and run out of the house and come back late. I would try to run outside too, but my father would grab me, beat me up, and sometimes lock me in. I don't know why they picked on me so much except that it just became the family habit to have *me* do everything for everyone. I was very lonely, I was never praised, and no matter what I tried to do, I was always told "no." I really felt bad about myself during those days. All I did was work, even though my parents worked on and off. My mother was a waitress, and my father was a taxi driver. Actually, they had and lost lots of jobs, so we were always worried about money around my house. They seemed taken up by a life that did not include us. My mother was mad at my father because of his other women, and my father hated my mother because she was always complaining. They didn't fight, but they didn't really get along. And we were best off to just stay out of their way. A few times they sent us away to live with our grandparents, because they couldn't afford to keep us. I was the one who held it together for my two sisters and my brother. But once we got separated, my parents were like strangers to us; they lived in another world, and we were on our own.

The white women remembered the adult women in their families as characteristically tired, busy, or sad. They recalled their mothers' lives as being full of drudgery, and for the most part, adult women were emotionally unavailable. As female children, these women did not work outside their homes to contribute to the family resource base, despite the fact that the families were sometimes very poor.

Gwen continued:

When I graduated from high school, I stayed at home and continued to take care of the house. I really wanted to get a job, but they needed me at home. We had boarders, so I had to do their dirty work too. I hated how mean they were to me, so when I met the boy who packed the groceries, I went to live with him at his house. My family was furious and began to chase and beat me—especially my father, who had to pick up some of the work around the house. I tried to explain that I would work and give them money, but they hated that I left. That's where I got this scar, from my father beating me up with a pipe when I refused to come home.

When all three groups were compared, the women's perceptions of the relationships between adult women and men in their households and community fell into a distinct pattern. Almost all of the women in the three sample groups felt as if their mothers or female caretakers considered their families havens from the harsh world of poverty and hard work, even those families whose domestic lives were characterized by economic difficulties, emotional distance, or physical abuse. As such, the women consistently attempted to create the image of a complete split between the public sphere and their private world, which, in many cases, influenced the gender roles of the women within their households of origin, making them more rigid and segregated.

The pattern of images the African American battered women recalled stand apart as being more complex than the other groups. They were less realistic, and they experienced a greater degree of contradictions between their thoughts and feelings. The women had more difficulty justifying their experiences with their desires than the other two groups.

ABUSE DURING CHILDHOOD

Early childhood victimization clearly emerged as a significant factor for a number of women in each of the three subgroups in this study, with eight women experiencing ongoing physical abuse as children, 13 sexual abuse, and 20 observing their mothers being abused. On this point, the subgroups had some experiences that were similar. In each case where there was violence in their childhood homes, the women were profoundly affected in some way. Those who were abused as children physically internalized the effects of childhood victimization, the feelings of worthlessness and betrayal, and the anxiety that resulted from living in constant fear. Some recalled blaming themselves for the abuse or feeling disdain from their abusive parent. Others described feeling shamed by the stigma associated with their traumatic involvements with child–protection services and juvenile–justice institutions, and being hurt by criticisms of their families from neighbors.

Witnessing maternal violence in their households of origin also affected the women in each subgroup of the sample. While some described concrete effects, such as homelessness, others described psychological consequences, such as depression. Most of the women who were abused as children and who witnessed maternal abuse believed that it significantly affected the nature of their self–definition and their attempts to create and maintain intimacy in their adult intimate relationships.

Angel, a twenty–two–year–old African American battered woman detained on a drug charge, said:

> I grew up with my brothers, my father, and my stepmother (who was much younger than my father) in public housing. We were very poor; my mother's public assistance and my father's disability weren't really enough to cover his medical care for his diabetes and amputated leg. It was a bad scene, lots of arguing and fighting. My father was a terror, and my brothers learned how to follow his lead—all of the men beat up females. When the boys dropped out of school and started selling drugs out of the apartment, my stepmom tried to get them to stop by calling the police. That's when they almost killed her. As for me, they used me for sex. At first it was only that they let their friends who used drugs in the house have me, but then they began to rape me themselves. My stepmother was afraid of them, and my father was getting sicker and stayed in bed drunk. I was only twelve years old. Oh yes, lots of people knew what was going on, but everyone was so afraid of my brothers that they didn't help. I was ashamed and embarrassed. I quit school at eighth grade and started hanging out. When one of my brothers was killed in a bad drug deal, my stepmother skipped town. With all of my protection gone, I ran away myself and started living on the streets,

boosting [shoplifting] with a group of girls that one of my brothers had introduced me to. They were the closest thing to family I
ever had. We took care of each other, but drugs just ran us into
the ground. Still, it was the closest thing to family I ever had.
Some of the girls are in [jail] with me now. It's good to be with
them again.

Of the twenty–six African American battered women, twelve
had been victims of sexual abuse and four were physically abused
as children. This relatively low rate of physical abuse may be related, in part, to the women's privileged positions in their households. Paradoxically, their vulnerability to and response to the
sexual abuse, in particular, was related to feeling "special."

As Melanie, a twenty–seven–year–old African American battered woman detained on a murder charge, said:

I felt terrible about my uncle fondling me. It made me feel like
dirt. But the way he described it, it was supposed to make me
feel special. I tried to think like that, but there was such a gap
between how I felt and what he was doing to me that I couldn't
stand it. But who could I tell? I knew that it would completely
tear my family apart, and that their opinion of *me* would change.
How could strong, smart, pretty me get myself into this mess?
It started out with him touching my privates, and putting his
fingers inside of me. Then he began to have sex with me in the
butt [anal intercourse]. The things he did to me were so bad that
there was no explanation that they could accept. So I just tried
to avoid him, but he didn't stop for the seven years that he lived
in our house. I was his "special friend," which means he raped
me on a regular basis, at least once a week.

Melanie, like other children in this sample who were sexually
abused, wanted very much to please the adult members of her
family. Because of her feeling pity for men in particular, and her
sense of herself as a powerful and privileged child, she was ironically laden with a feeling that the sexual abuse was, as Melanie
stated, "my burden to bear," an interpretation that furthered the
women's vulnerability to gender entrapment.

When the African American battered women observed violence toward adult women in their families, it was seldom spo-
ken about, and was more tolerated than in the other groups of

women I interviewed. The response to abuse was significant because in most *other* instances, the children and adults openly discussed their feelings and problems. Unlike their other childhood experiences, in this situation, the women described feeling helpless, not powerful.

For instance, Kim, a thirty–seven–year old African American battered woman detained on a prostitution charge, said:

> I could never understand why my mother didn't just ask me for help. I helped her with everything else she couldn't handle. It wasn't as if I didn't know what was going on; it was more like she didn't think it mattered that this man was beating her. I felt sorry for her, and I also felt helpless as a child. After a beating, she would hold me and cry and say things like "you must remember that your father loves you and that we are a family." It was like she just couldn't leave him.

Only one woman whose mother was abused recalled her parents' relationship ending. The others felt that their mothers, aunts, and sisters who experienced violence felt compelled to tolerate it and respond in an uncritical manner that was consistent with the value of being loyal to, and hence trapped within, their families.

The childhood abuse experiences of African American women who were not battered as adults fell into a household pattern: all of the children were abused rather than it being an isolated experience for a particular child, as was true for the African American women who were battered. While the abuse was traumatic, it did not have the paradoxical effect it had on the battered African American women, whose privileged status or unique role worked against them.

Gloria reported:

> As kids, we were all abused. It was just the way it was in our house. It was usually when he [her father] was drunk, and he would hit us with his belt or crack our heads against the wall. He was known for throwing things—big things—across the room at us when he got mad or upset about something. My brothers, sisters and I were really very scared of my father, but we could at least stick together when he came after us. When my brothers got older, they would fight back at him, and eventually he stopped abusing even us younger kids.

In the group of African American women who were not battered, the women reported that they witnessed their mothers being emotionally abused by the male adults in the families more than physically abused. In those cases where maternal physical abuse *did* occur in their households, the pattern suggested less tolerance and more rapid resolution because their mothers terminated the relationship.

Gloria, a forty–two–year–old African American woman detained on drug charges, said:

> One thing I learned from my mother was to never let a man touch me. I'm telling you, when he went upside her head, she went right back at him with a frying pan. It was really scary because he was so much stronger than she was, but she knew how to use anything she could get her hands on as a weapon. After a few months of that mess, she just packed us up and left him. It was hard for awhile because we had to move around a lot, but I knew that we had to go. My mama told me that she would have killed him otherwise.

All of the white battered women in this study were physically and sexually abused as children. They described experiences that were particularly horrific; the violence was more severe, and the families were more isolated, than in the other two subgroups. They were also neglected as children.

As Clara, a forty–five–year–old woman detained on a drug charge, said:

> I was the oldest kid in my family. Both of my parents were drunks, so that meant I had to take care of my brother and sister from the time I was about six. I loved them and remember pretending like I was their mother. They were very attached to me, and I liked that they depended on me. I did the best I could to protect them from the life my parents were leading. They were very abusive; beatings happened on a regular basis in my house. My mother beat us and my father beat everyone. It was common. Also there was never enough food. My relationships with my brother and sister was the best relationship I have ever had. . . . Nothing has ever felt like love to me except that. But I had no friends or support. I was a twelve–year–old adult, and it all fell apart one day when my sister turned over a pot of boiling water and was burned over ninety percent of her body. I was

supposed to be watching her. My parents were out drinking and my brother was wet, but we were out of diapers. I was trying to figure out what to do, and I left her too long in the kitchen alone. I just couldn't be everywhere at once. When my mother came home, they had taken all of us away. My sister was in the hospital, where she stayed for over a year, and my brother and I were at the police station. I was put in a foster home, but I kept running away to find my brother and sister. I ended up in a state facility. My mother never got custody back. I don't really know if she ever tried. I lost contact with my brother, and I've seen my sister once in the past thirty years. I was a big fat disappointment to every one who needed and loved me. I've been looking for a family ever since.

These women observed their mothers both physically and emotionally abused, and, like the African American women who were battered later in life, the white women's mothers generally did not terminate their abusive relationships. However, these women explained their mothers' tolerance for the abuse in terms of their mothers' isolation and limited options, rather than loyalty, as the African American battered women did. A few of the white women's mothers even left, but eventually returned to the abusive relationships because they could not manage on their own, given the lack of services available to battered women prior to the 1970s. Chris, age twenty–four, detained on charges of robbery and possession of stolen property, said:

Where would my mother have gone? Yes, he was awful to her and to us. She was beaten so badly that she would have black eyes all of the time. He'd tie her to a chair and if she cried he'd stuff a rag in her mouth. We'd try to help but then he'd beat us too. She'd try to make us not get involved, but we were the only ones who could have saved her at that time.... She didn't have any family or friends...he made sure of that. And she could have never taken care of us alone. For her, I guess staying was the only option she thought she had. There was no such thing as a battered woman those days.... Only some women had bad home lives, that's all.

As the previous accounts illustrate, the incidence and response to experiences or observation of abuse during childhood are significant for gender entrapment. The findings indicated that the meanings, rationalizations, and explanations the adult women offered about abuse to their children both influenced and were influenced by their loyalty to their families, particularly to the social position of men. Whether they decided to leave or stay, their willingness or ability to use public services, and where they placed the blame for abuse influenced the women's patterns of response to violence as adults. The African American battered women were most often socialized to excuse or tolerate violence from men, and learned that loyalty and stability, in most instances, were paramount to their own safety and satisfaction.

VULNERABILITY, RISK-TAKING, AND FEAR OF SUCCESS

Many of the women in all three groups described themselves as "risk-takers," but the context and result of their risk-taking differed in ways that are important to the theoretical model of gender entrapment. As previously noted, some of the African American women who were battered recalled feeling ambivalent about the public and household recognition that accompanied being exceptional. Consequently, some behaved in ways that limited or denied opportunities for their advancement so that they would not "stand out" or harm relationships with their siblings, peers, and potential mates. The various manifestations of this ambivalence indicate the many ways that being a child with a sense of personal power, self-pride, and opportunity was compromised by the effects of growing up as a girl, poor, and African American in contemporary society. For, despite their sense of self-esteem that originated from their positions in their families or households, they encountered obstacles in the public world that left them feeling out of place or "weird."

As Blondie, a twenty-one-year-old African American battered woman detained on a felonious drug charge, stated:

> When I was young, I thought I'd have a great life. I felt like I was going to be able to run with the wind, to take risks and succeed—surprising the world with myself. I dreamed that I would have a companion relationship with someone like my mom. She and I were very close, and I liked the kind of person that she was. When she got sick with a bad heart, I had to leave school to work. Our church was helpful to us for a while, but we became

poor very fast. I started working at a clothing store and taking
care of my two baby sisters. At work they treated me like a
slave, which I just wasn't used to. I kept trying to act like I was
as honest, hardworking and important as my family taught me I
was, but when they accused me of stealing, it was over. They
said someone had seen a Black girl leaving the store with some
boxes of merchandise, and it *had* to be me or one of my friends. I
quit that job, but things like that just kept happening to me. I'm
not saying I was perfect, but I am no thief. I got real depressed
real fast. I lost my way when I realized that I couldn't risk just
running with the wind.

The frustration of "bumping up against limits" (Lynne, age
twenty–eight) resulted in the women "holding themselves back"
(Beverly, age thirty–three) in order to be more acceptable. Some
of the African American battered women in this group began engaging in activities that they knew would result in negative sanctions when, having emerged from their protected households,
they were told or treated as if they could not excel in school.
Others felt that sexual abuse or harassment in their workplace
limited their options for success in the world.
Blondie continued:

I was much too energetic, too smart and too good for the people I
worked for. And when one of my bosses tried to get it on with
me, I quit. He followed me one night and raped me in his car just
before I left. I was hurt, but I wouldn't let him stop me. Instead,
I stopped myself. I started hanging out with a group of people
who were no good for me. Actually, they were fun and smart too,
but they weren't into anything positive. But I thought it was
easier not to try and fail again. It was a control thing...like no
one was going to get me down but myself. Not to mention the
fact that the money selling drugs was good, fast, and it helped
me take care of my mom, until I got into heavy using.

Blondie's story illustrates a common theme that was significant to the gender entrapment of the African American battered
women. Their families had very high expectations, and the wom-
en were afraid of failing them. For the women, the risk–taking
was associated with behavior that seemed to sabotage their success. As a result of this frustration, some became emotionally de-

tached teen–agers. In each of these cases, the women felt the limiting boundaries of expected gender behavior and racial/ethnic stereotypes very clearly, and most modified their childhood aspirations and subsequent behavior to stay within these boundaries.

For example, Beverly, a thirty–three–year–old woman detained on a burglary charge, said:

> It was clear to me very early that the only way to have a man was to be a superwoman, but not let the man know. It happened over and over. In some ways, it was like acting. My mother gave my father her paycheck so it looked like he had a job. In school, I acted like I wasn't so smart and like I needed boys' help to fix my bicycle. I stopped playing sports when my father stopped taking me fishing with him because I was a girl.... That hurt me. I also started to act like I liked having sex even though I didn't, and then I got pregnant because *he* wanted a son. It has all been a big act, but I felt pressured into it because I didn't know any other girls like me, and my family expected me to be perfect... to become the perfect lady.

The African American women who were not battered described similar behaviors that could be considered risk–taking, only with more obvious negative consequences. However, unlike the African American battered women, the women in this subgroup reported that they did not temper their actions based on a sense that they needed to fit into a set gender role. They felt that their behavior was less regulated by social or family expectation, emphasizing instead the importance of peer relationships as a key source of their identities. Even though the women in this subgroup anticipated negative social consequences for both acting out *and* assuming entitled positions, they did not let the fear of negative sanctions inhibit their positive or negative activities.

Letoya, age twenty–six, detained on a drug charge, said:

> I never felt like I could be the kind of girl my friends were anyway, so I just decided to be myself. I watched my two sisters and two brothers, and I watched my mother and father. I realized that the best way to get out of the house was to act like a boy, which meant doing boy–like things... not listening, fighting,

breaking rules in school. I got a job after school packing groceries, and that was my ticket to freedom. Oh, I liked pretty dresses and to have my hair done, but I knew that would never get me anywhere. I just had to follow my own lead, even though it landed me in some bad places...like Rikers Island.

Like Letoya, the women in this subgroup were generally active in their risk–taking behavior, initiating socially unacceptable activities and offering leadership in such activities to their peers. In this way, the African American women who were not battered reported a pattern of behavior that was *not* within conventional gender–role expectations.

The white battered women in this study described behavior intended to avoid taking risks, choosing instead to behave in ways that characteristically were attempts to survive as female children with lower status in their families. They worked to *avoid* rejection by parents, siblings, and peers, indicating a more passive or compliant motivation for entering into relationships and engaging in certain activities.

Shirley, a forty–three–year–old woman detained on a drug–possession charge, said:

I was never a risk–taker, except to please others. We had very clear rules in my family. But we were also very poor, and I thought that it would help if I could bring in some money. I had a lot of different schemes. I would lie about my age and get a job until my parents found out that I wasn't at school. Or I would steal clothes and sell them...or sometimes I'd keep some for my brother and I to wear to school. At one point, I thought that helping my brother do well in school would be the way to help us out, so I started doing all of his homework for him. I always had a plan, but, in the end, it didn't seem to help me or my family very much.

For different reasons, the white battered women and the African American battered women characteristically had few close friends and were driven to behave in ways that they felt were in concert with social values and expectations. The African American women who were not battered were more interested in peer–defined success and were less vulnerable to parental or social rejection. In this way, the three subgroups in this sample were distinctly different from each other; the African American battered women were most likely to censor themselves and in some instances to sabotage their chances of success in response to social and/or peer rejection.

As Blondie said:

> I dropped out of the world because the world wasn't ready for me yet. Dropping out was better than falling off or being thrown away. At least I could fool myself into thinking I was still in control of my family life. So I dropped out and into my man's lap—ready to live out my dreams there instead.

DREAMS OF ADULT RELATIONSHIPS

As previously discussed, most of the families of the women in all three subgroups in this study were not structurally or functionally consistent with the dominant hegemonic norm of the heterosexual, nuclear, middle–class family. Even so, the women were influenced by the broader ideology of the social world outside of their families, and their experiences were shaped by social structures and values beyond their communities. This influence was most evident in the women's dreams about marriage and family life, their role models, and the distinct ways that the three groups responded to their divergence from the ideological norm.

Most of the African American battered women strongly desired a traditional nuclear family. Even though this did not necessarily reflect the reality of their childhood experiences, most desired a life as adult women that included a "very romantic" relationship with a man (Grace, age thirty–eight), "lots of affection and attention" (April, age twenty–one), and the opportunity "to stay at home with my children" (Vernice, age forty–three).

Lynne, age twenty–eight, detained on a drug charge, said:

> I remember wanting a kind, sweet husband when I grew up; someone who I could reach out for my dreams with, just the two of us. It would be very different from my mother and father. I wanted more romance, intimacy, and affection. A fuller, more loving life. He'd be in charge, and I'd follow his lead. I was a kingmaker at heart. It was my life dream to support a strong man.

On the one hand, the women's descriptions of their desires

sounded conventional in nature. On the other hand, it included a subtext that was centered on an awareness of structural barriers to their achieving this goal.

Lynne continued:

> That would mean that racism would have to end so that my man would be able to get a job. If *I* stayed at home I would not have been an average housewife. I planned to go to school and get a degree so that I could teach my kids at home. That would be better for them than the lousy schools in this city that do everything they can to keep Black folks down, dumb, and depressed.

The role models identified by the African American battered women were consistent with these fantasies. "I'd be a tough cookie, only loving, sexy and funny, like Mae West," said Kim, age thirty–seven, or "I'd be like Nina Simone because she's dark, strong *and* beautiful.... Most strong, dark women aren't considered beautiful in this culture, but I grew up thinking I would change that," said Sylvia, age twenty–eight.

The African American women who were not battered were the most likely of the three subgroups in this study to identify their mothers or other female caretakers as their role models, not with reverence, but with a sense of realism. They generally expressed a closer, more compassionate feeling for the adult women in their lives, and felt they wanted to and, in fact, would grow up to be very much like them.

The women in this group did not feel that marriage to a man would necessarily provide positive rewards for them. They expressed the hope that they would meet someone and fall in love, but they denied the expectation that they would actually be or stay married. They did not feel that a relationship with a man would produce structural changes from the lives they knew as children. For some, their discussion took on a distinctly feminist tone. Jackie, age thirty–seven, said, "I don't need a man to make me happy."

Two women in this group were identified as lesbians or expressed an interest in establishing long–term relationships with women. Terry, a twenty–six–year–old African American woman detained on a drug charge, said:

> The best, or I should say the only good relationship that I have

ever had was with my current lover.... She's waiting for me on the outside. I tried being with men because I thought I was supposed to, but I've known for a long time I was sexually interested in women, not men. Once I came to realize that men couldn't even provide for me in the world, I asked myself, "Why even be with men?" I might as well be happy with a woman, which I am.

The white battered women had the most difficulty identifying women role models. Their life stories were markedly void of women whom they admired. The white women identified men as role models even though the question was posed in gender-specific terms: "Tell me about the women you think of as role models; who did you look up to or admire?" Four did not answer or responded like Shirley, age forty–three, detained for drug possession: "I just wanted a chance to be myself, or I thought I was going to be different from everyone I knew." The white women from the most violent families responded with some version of "I didn't look up to anyone."

The women in this group strongly identified with the values and hegemonic images of marriage, but their memories of childhood did not characteristically include a sense of their abilities to imagine such a life for themselves. They reported feeling worried and frustrated about not knowing how to attain their dreams for the future; most felt like marriage *should* offer an escape from the dreary life to which they were accustomed. They felt pressure to "find the right man" a feat that, by their accounts, few of the women they knew, including their mothers, had been able to do.

Margaret, a twenty–seven–year–old white woman who was battered for three years by her boyfriend and then arrested for harassing him, said:

In some ways the problem was that I chose the wrong man. How he turned things against me so fast, I don't know. But I do believe that somewhere out there is a man who will deliver me to that spot where I'd be well taken care of at last. He'd be different from my father, and different from any boyfriend I've had so far... but he must be out there somewhere. It's a constant search for women like me to find the right man. It's just part of our life as females.

HOW LIFE WOULD HAVE BEEN DIFFERENT
IF THEY'D BEEN BOYS

Most of the women in each of the three groups felt that their lives would have been very different if they'd been male. All of the respondents felt that, in retrospect, being female children in their families and in the world outside of their households was a significant factor in creating negative experiences in their lives. The distinction between the three subgroups was that this awareness came to them at distinctly different times in their lives.

The African American battered women characteristically responded to this question in abstract, philosophical terms: "I would have had the freedom to choose my life path more freely," said Melanie, age twenty–seven. Almost all of them answered this question hesitantly, and with considerable ambivalence, especially those who had higher levels of privilege in their households. In most cases, awareness of the social liability that gender created for them was associated with critical negative experiences that came later in the women's lives from the world *outside* their families of origin. Most of these felt that they would have been able to take fuller advantage of their relative household privilege, actualizing their identities as "favored children" into being powerful, successful adults if they'd been boys.

Lois, age fifty–four, charged with prostitution, said:

> If I was a boy, I would be more aggressive than I am, and I wouldn't have to hold in the pent–up energy I can't express. I would have taken better care of myself because I would have demanded more. I would not have had as much work to do just to stay alive. I would have worked to make myself successful. You know what? I wouldn't have been arrested for prostitution. First of all, I wasn't soliciting when the cops picked me up, and second of all, if I was, I sure would make more money as a male prostitute than a female! I'd be an all–around more successful person no matter *what* I did.

The responses from the African American women who were not battered varied, but typically were concrete in nature. "I would not have the nine children that I do," said Lenore, age twenty–seven, or "I'd have had more flexibility to work in a high–paying job, like as a plumber," said Gloria, age forty–two.

Like the African American women who were battered, they seemed to have a more recent awareness of gender liability based on adolescent or adult experiences rather than circumstances of their childhoods. They made a distinction between being a girl— a neutral category for them—and being a woman, a member of a dominated group whose status was precarious.

Anita, age thirty–five, detained on a drug charge, said:

> In general being a girl was a breeze. It was nice.... I liked it a lot. But being a grown lady is a total drag. All it means is working much more than men, having to please others rather than yourself and being left. I'm telling you, things need to change for it to be all right to be a woman today. But being a girl was as good a way to grow up as any.

The battered white women, who characteristically experienced less privileged status within their households, unilaterally felt that the burden and limitations associated with being adult women began for them with the burden of being girls in their households of origin.

Linda, age thirty–three, detained on a felony drug charge, said:

> My mother and I would just look at each other with sad eyes. Sometimes we'd hold hands, but we didn't talk much. I think it was because we were both just so tired for all we had to do. It was the one female connection, being sad together. The boys had a good life, and, yes, if I was a boy I would not have been so tired then or so sad just like I am now.

While all the women I interviewed described how their current lives would be different if their early childhood experiences had been similar to that of their male siblings, all also initiated comments during the life–history interviews that indicated that they enjoyed some aspects of being female. Most of them felt compelled to clarify a misconception that *I* as an interviewer might come to: that they had *wished* they were boys and would become boys if they could. Indeed, while most of them believed that being female was an impediment to their life chances as children or adults, they reported that they were glad to be women. They generally appreciated women more then men, and those who had daughters liked them better than their sons.

"My girls are my pride and joy; the boys are too rough for me," said Carolyn, age thirty. "I 'm pregnant now and I hope I have a girl, I never want to have a son," said Kim, age thirty–seven. "Whatever you do, get a woman lawyer and judge; they are just more honest," said Aisha, age twenty–six. "Some of the girls here are great. Even though I'm mad as hell at my co–defendant for turning me in, she and the other girls I worked with on the outside are the best family I have ever had, and we hang tough with each other," said Blondie, age twenty–one. "I love women. We are stronger and more honest. As soon as I get out of here, I'm going to be a woman again—that means staying off drugs," said Toni, age thirty–three.

RACIAL/ETHNIC IDENTITY AND FAMILY LOYALTY

Both subgroups of African American women used repeated references to their race/ethnicity during the interview as a way to establish a frame of reference about community norms, family values, and their experiences in the social world. Their ideas and behavior were shaped by an awareness of the current and historical position of their particular racial/ethnic group within the larger social structure.

For the African American battered women, a sense of racial/ethnic identity and family loyalty had a contradictory effect on their identities similar to the contradiction of gender and role privilege, all key elements of gender entrapment. On the one hand, feeling what could be described as an almost universal connection to African American people and a deep sense of cultural pride was empowering and helped to create a cohesive family unit for these women.

Sebina, age thirty, charged with co–conspiracy to murder, said:

We were one of those proud Black families. No one in our family went without if we had something to share. And by family I mean lots of people who we loved, for you see, it was drilled into us that we had to take care of our own and that is the only reason we are around as Black people today. I loved that feeling about us. You should have seen holidays around our place— cooking for days, lots of people, looking at photo albums, and remembering Aunt what's–her–name.

Or, as Carolyn, age thirty, detained on a murder charge, said:

> Black people are the best. You know, we are strong, honest, and
> will overcome any obstacle in our way. Sometimes we lose our
> way, but as people we are solid as a rock.

At the same time, however, this sense of racial solidarity served
to limit the women's self determination, independence, and autonomy, leaving them vulnerable to the gender entrapment that
resulted in violence from their male partners and subsequent
participation in illegal activities. In retrospective descriptions,
the African American battered women excused the negative actions of men in their lives because of the harsh realities of
African American life in this country, while they held the
women, including themselves, to a higher standard. Family loyalty took on this exaggerated meaning because the women felt
that African American families historically were discredited because of how their families contradicted the hegemonic norm—
the relative economic power of African American women when
compared to African American men. In many cases, the African
American battered women felt that in contemporary social life it
was actually African American *men* who were the scapegoats of
the historical legacy of slavery and, as such, they were, as Melanie, twenty–seven, put it, the "true sufferers of racial inequality." "Our families are only as strong as the weakest member,
who today is the Black man," said Letisha, age thirty–seven. Historically based loyalty to family, therefore, got constructed as
contemporary loyalty to *men*.

The responses from each of the non–battered African American women differed from the battered women in that their loyalties were less focused on their particular families, per se, but
more on African American people in general. The nature of their
expressions of their racial/ethnic identities did not have the
same element of pride or historical references. Rather, they took
on a more contemporary, fatalistic tone. The elements of cultural solidarity they emphasized were the experiences of mutual
oppression that women and men faced. For example, they felt
like Toni, age thirty–three, who said:

> It's bad for Black people—men, women, and children. Nothing
> can help, not with all the drugs and crime. My family has been
> poor forever, and we always will be.

The white battered women in this study did not reveal strong racial/ethnic identities, even when probed. In each case, their family loyalties were expressed in more obligatory then prideful ways, and did not include a consideration of historical circumstances or community solidarity. Linda, age thirty–three, detained on a sexual–harassment charge, said:

> Well of course I have a strong identity to my family. No matter how bad it was, they are still my family, and I must have gotten something from them. We did not really have a race or anything like that. I know that sounds funny, but we were just regular Christian white people…and we weren't either proud nor ashamed of that. Until now, I never really thought about it.

CONCLUSION: GENDER ENTRAPMENT AND THE HOUSEHOLDS OF ORIGIN

Several features generally characterize all of the families of origin of the three subgroups in this study. Despite slight variations in income level, all of the women's families lived close to the social and economic margin. Even those women who described their lives as "comfortable" experienced their economic status as fragile. Most of the families depended on multiple incomes from unstable jobs to support the family, and even those who accumulated extra material possessions were vulnerable to changes in employment status, health problems, and other unexpected family crises. In both subgroups of African American women, the women's mothers worked outside of the homes, while the white women did so only on occasion. In all of the families, the women were primary caretakers of the children, and all of the women worked in their households, performing routine household tasks that were usually organized around gender. Only the white families were highly organized by generation; in the African American families the distinctions between children and adults were less rigid.

Of the seven themes that emerged about the families, childhood roles, and the construction of female identities, the findings indicated that the three subgroups interviewed in this study were distinct. The African American women who were battered were distinguished by their racial/ethnic identity and by their early childhood experiences. The variation on seven features illuminates the gender entrapment that the African American battered women experienced.

• In terms of their positions in their households, the African American battered women described childhoods that were distinguished from other childhoods by more privileges, material possessions, and attention. With this elevated status came a symbolic burden on the women to *maintain* the privileged status through emotional, academic, household, and other "work." This unusual position and their efforts to maintain status were the initial circumstance that left the African American battered women vulnerable to gender entrapment.

In contrast, the African American women who were not battered recalled being average children, feeling a sense of commonality with the other children with whom they grew up. As such, they were less concerned with differentiating themselves from others. Of the three groups, the white children typically described childhood experiences that were the most deprived relative to other children in their families. They tended to be scapegoated and ignored, and their burdens were more concrete than emotional in nature. They almost came to expect degrading treatment and recognized it quickly as such.

• The second theme that emerged from the data as an important finding for the gender–entrapment theory was the images the women had of adult women and men. The African American battered women recalled a paradoxical relationship with their female caretakers. On the one hand, they tended to idealize them, and, on the other hand, they described feeling distant and, at times, disappointed in their mothers' lack of emotional and physical availability to them as children. The African American battered women adopted their mothers' tendency to feel sorry for men in their lives, tolerating their irresponsibility, their limitations, their indiscretions, and, ultimately, their violence, as the following chapter will show.

The African American women who were not battered had a more realistic sense of who their mothers were. This subgroup tended to identify with their mothers in more ways than the African American battered women, including taking on their mothers' dismissal or disdain for men. Their mothers were less generous with their tolerance and more discounting of men's roles in their lives. In this way, they were significantly less vulnerable to men's violence as adults. The white women were generally more distant from adults as children than the other two groups, and they tended to feel sorry for their mothers and to avoid interaction with their fathers. However, as children, the white battered women developed an understanding of the relative power that men and boys held in their families and, indeed, in the world.

• The findings from this theme were related to a third theme that emerged from the data as relevant to gender entrapment: the women's experiences and observation of abuse during their childhood. In each subgroup, the women tended to internalize and draw meaning from their mothers' responses to abuse if they observed it. The African American battered women's mothers who were battered themselves tended not to leave abusive relationships, while the African American non–battered women's mothers tended to resist and leave right away. The white women's mothers responded to being abused by planning to leave and attempting to leave. However, in the end, they were not able to stay away permanently for a number of reasons. In each case, the decision to stay or to leave was related to the mother's sense of herself in relationship to the man by whom she was abused, as well as the availability of concrete options.

For those women in this study who themselves experienced abuse as children, the effect was significant, albeit different, for each subgroup. The African American battered women were less often physically abused as children and more often abused sexually, which is a significant element in their gender entrapment. The role of protecting the adults who committed this heinous act was added to the burden of being "special" children and had, therefore, a particularly confusing and troubling consequence for the abused children. The African American non–battered women experienced some physical and sexual abuse, but were not targeted as victims any more than other children in their families, as the African American battered women were. All of the white women in this sample were abused as children, and, like the African American battered women, internalized some of the consequences. For them, the situation was compounded by serious childhood neglect.

• As the African American battered women grew up and began to encounter the subtle messages and overt pressures from the social world to conform to "appropriate" gender and racial/ethnic roles, they began to engage in self–limiting behavior in order to more consistently fit within their sense of expected behaviors. The African American battered women were surprised that they did not command the same respect from teachers, employers, and peers that they did from their families, and they began to work even harder to please others rather than themselves. They tended to avoid risks, and some even sabotaged their opportunities for social advancement. Instead, they focused on their domestic relationships, becoming overconfident of their abilities to effect change in the private sphere of their lives.

At the other extreme from the African American battered women, the African American non–battered women in the sample were the most likely to ignore expectations and to take symbolic and concrete risks while they were growing up. When they felt discriminatory treatment in the public or private sphere that limited their choices or constricted their behavior, they defied regulations despite the threat of punishment. The women in this subgroup were much more peer–identified than the other two groups, and they did not censor themselves. Instead, they sometimes acted incautiously and engaged in behaviors that resulted in negative sanctions. The white battered women in the sample tried to avoid rejection, as did the African American battered women, but they had come to expect it and had learned to cope more effectively with it. As children and young women they broke rules only to advance their status in their families, motivated by external rather than internal interests and needs.

• All of the women in this study initially desired traditional, heterosexual nuclear families, especially the African American battered women. In this subgroup, the women's motivations were, in part, in response to their sense of family loyalty, their sense of family life needing strong women (such as the ones they thought they would become), and their desire to rest and be taken care of in response to negative experiences in the public sphere, which they felt was hostile to them.

The African American women who were not battered also wanted family lives that were consistent with the dominant form; however, they expressed a pessimistic view of the likelihood that they would be able to accomplish this goal. The non–battered African American women abandoned their desire to fit the ideological norm at a very early age. They were prepared to have their relationships fail and were open and willing to establish alternative family forms.

The white women remained highly attached to the dominant ideology about family, and they imagined that the hegemonic family would answer the problems they faced as relatively deprived children. The dreams of the women in this subgroup had an escapist tone. These findings are relevant to the gender–entrapment theoretical model inasmuch as the African American battered women worked the hardest and the longest and, indeed, with the most conviction, to create and maintain a hegemonic nuclear family, even when the violence began and they became involved in illegal activities.

• The meaning of the women's gender roles, as expressed through the question, "How would your life have been different were you a boy?" was consistent with the overall patterns that emerged from the three subgroups. African American or white, all of the women felt that their lives had been negatively influenced by the constraints placed on them because of their gender. The differences among the three subgroups lay in the developmental stage and in the social moment that the women *felt* the gender constraints. The African American battered women felt vulnerable as women but not as girls. Their experiences of gender were distinguished from the other groups as more abstract. This finding was ironic given the extent of sexual abuse they experienced. It suggested how significant denial was to their gender entrapment, for even as young girls the women sensed that by sacrificing themselves, they were serving a greater cause in their families—men's need for power, the sexual satisfaction of their abuser or preserving the families' integrity by not disclosing the abuse.

The African American women who were not battered expressed awareness of a more concrete set of limiting factors that were gender related. The white battered women also acknowledged their gender liability in concrete terms; however, their consciousness of limitations began much earlier in their lives than for either subgroup of African American women.

• The last theme that emerged from the life–history interviewes about the women's families of origin that is relevant to the gender–entrapment theoretical model was the importance of racial/ethnic identity and solidarity in the women's overall sense of themselves. As the cases illustrated, the African American women in both groups expressed a keener sense of their racial/ethnic identity than the white battered women. However, for the African American battered women, loyalty was directed to their families and, by implication, to African American men in their families. This factor was a key element in their emotional interest, everyday work, and identities as "Black women trying to create families with Black men," which was changing to "battered women," "victim," or "female offenders." In contrast, the African American women who were not battered constructed their racial/ethnic identities more in terms of the African American community as a whole, including African American women. They consider the contemporary issues that limit women's lives as central and important. Their identities were less gender–bound and relationship–bound. The white battered women did not indicate that race/ethnicity was a critical element of their identities, and it did not overtly influence their behaviors, thoughts, or feelings as much as it did the African American battered women.

The seven themes comprise the significant elements of gender entrapment in terms of identity development. The experiences and perceptions of the women in the three subgroups varied considerably, indicating three distinct patterns in the overall population of women I interviewed. The emphasis on the childhood experiences of the African American battered women—their relatively privileged household status, their culturally constructed loyalty, their families' expectation of them, their dreams, and their vulnerabilities as they grew up as African American girl–children in contemporary society—point to the ways they were *uniquely* positioned to experience gender entrapment.

4

TRAPPED BY VIOLENCE

"Just trying to deal with the force of his blows"

THE WOMEN'S experiences of violence in their adult intimate relationships are the second category of critical experiences in gender entrapment. The findings reported in this chapter primarily concern the experiences of the two subgroups of battered women. The third subgroup—African American women who were not battered—will be discussed to illustrate a contrast where relevant.

By comparing these subgroups, the emotional, cultural, and social factors that distinguish the African American battered women's experiences as gender entrapment are illuminated. While it is important to reiterate that the literature on battering does not indicate a significant discrepancy on the rate of violence within different racial/ethnic groups, *experiential* nuances do vary by race/ethnicity. The nature of these differences form a distinct pattern that are essential elements in the theoretical model of gender entrapment.

The pattern that emerged from the findings consisted of variation on three sequential aspects of the women's experiences: 1) the circumstantial and emotional factors that created the women's vulnerability to abuse from their male partners, 2) the consequences of the physical, emotional and sexual abuse in their intimate relationships, and 3) the women's response to the violence. The variations constitute a pattern that created the opportunity for intimate violence and explains why, when it occurred, some women could not or chose not to leave their intimate relationships, despite the horrific consequences of abuse. The analysis of the findings showed that the African American battered women, in particular, stayed in abusive relationships until it was too late to get out. By then they were virtually trapped by their gender identity, by their socially constructed loyalty to the African American men, and ultimately by the violence itself.

CIRCUMSTANTIAL AND EMOTIONAL VULNERABILITY TO ABUSE

The women whose stories are told in this book described a range of characteristics and experiences that left them more or less vulnerable to physical, emotional, and sexual abuse in their intimate relationships. The distinctions between the subgroups revealed a pattern that varied by race/ethnicity, pointing to the paradoxical ways that the gender–identity development in the household of origin of the African American battered women converged with their socially constructed loyalty to African American men and their disappointing experiences in the public sphere to create circumstancial and emotional vulnerability to abuse. This vulnerability was an essential element in their gender entrapment.

The findings indicate that the white battered women and the African American non–battered women had very different circumstances and emotional responses to their adult relationships with men. Consequently, their experiences and the meaning they attached to events in the private sphere of their lives were inconsistent with the gender–entrapment theoretical model.

The "Wonderful" Early Days

For most of the African American battered women, their intimate relationships with the men who later abused them were initially positive and mutually satisfying. Typically the violence began after the second year of being together. The African American battered women denied to themselves and others that a dangerous pattern was emerging in their domestic lives; they generally considered the violent episodes an aberration of their male partners' otherwise tolerable—and sometimes even pleasant— behavior.

Cheryl, a thirty–two–year–old African American woman detained on a prostitution charge, was abused by her husband for twelve years. She said:

> It was hard to figure out what was going on at first. He was the father of my kids, and very proud to be with me. Everything was so wonderful in the early days; our life was beautiful. I was so happy that he chose me because he had lots of ladies around him. We were real sweethearts; he gave me gifts and showed a lot of respect for me. By being with him, I became softer, although he first fell for my assertive, funny, more strong side. He gave me a chance to be quiet and taken care of, and that was real nice for me. He was working at Con Edison, and I was at the phone company at the time. Our little apartment in Harlem was a sweet, quiet place. We'd have my family over and they envied me. . . . They didn't believe that I'd ever make such a gentle wife. I think our problems started when he lost his job. He acted like *I* was the one who was out of work. He blamed his failure on me, that I was putting too much pressure on him and all. But it was really him. Maybe I smothered him too much. Or maybe he went crazy. All I know is that there was something that turned this dream into the biggest nightmare of my life. The only thing I can say now is that trying to change for someone else is a very big mistake.

As Cheryl's story illustrates, the shift in the nature of the relationships was typically gradual. In some cases, the African American battered women realistically attributed the shift to external events, such as the man's loss of a job, a change in the household's financial status, or the onset of alcohol or drug use. Given their marginalized social status, events like these were common for the young African American men, and served to mask the emerging abusive nature of their relationships.

Preoccupied with the negative social circumstances, and deeply loyal to the African American men, the African American battered women felt compelled, as twenty–year–old April said, to "comfort, advise, and support their men like any good wife would." The combination of a pleasant early relationship, the gradual nature of the onset of abuse, and the discouraging incidents in the couples' lives left the African American battered women distracted and vulnerable to accelerating male violence.

In contrast, the white battered women felt less initial satisfaction from their relationships. They typically recalled fewer pleasant experiences even in the beginning, and they felt generally less emotionally engaged with their male partner than the African American battered women did. The white battered women had a pessimistic outlook; they did not expect that their relationships would provide them a sense of personal fulfillment or satisfaction. They entered relationships with men to be socially acceptable, not for their own happiness or sense of purpose. Their male partners did not experience as much failure in the public sphere as the African American men did, and the white battered women did not expend energy providing emotional support to them. These circumstances and the white battered women's emotions were important factors that protected them from gender entrapment; for even at the onset of the abuse, they were more detached from their relationships with the violent men in their lives than the African American battered women were.

"He Was One of Those Pitiful Men."

The African American battered women initially felt sorry for the men who abused them. Their historically superior status as privileged girls led them to rationalize and deny the seriousness of their upsetting domestic realities. The African American battered women were initially unable to incorporate their vulnerability to violence from their male partners into their self–perceptions, and so their vulnerability increased. They optimistically relied on the sense of personal power that resulted from their elevated status in their families of origin to get them through, and they maintained a commitment and loyalty to the African American men who were becoming abusive. Their initial tolerance and rationalization for their male partners' violence, and their generous, apathetic responses led some of them to feel sorry for their abusers rather than being fearful, resentful, or becoming angry with them.

Beverly, a thirty–three–year–old African American woman who was detained on a burglary charge, was battered for fourteen years by her common–law husband. She said:

> He was one of those pitiful men. He would really lay into me,
> and hurt me bad. It wasn't every day, but at times it was as
> much as once a week that he'd jump on me and start pushing,
> hitting, scratching, and insulting me. He was out of control, and
> I'd just try to stay calm. Honestly? I felt sorry for him. He was a
> real loser under it all. He couldn't keep a job, he didn't have
> family to speak of or another place to go. He'd call me up crying
> his eyes out, begging me to let him in, and I'd forgive him. He
> needed me, and I knew that. Not only didn't he have any mon-
> ey, he didn't have any sense. He was insecure, no skills, and ac-
> tually very pitiful. He comes from a troubled family, no sense of
> home training or pride. He's smart, but hasn't had much chance
> for improving himself. His father was a loser, his brothers are all
> crack–heads, and his mother really hated herself and her life.
> When you get a start like that, what can you do? That's why I
> was trying to bring him along...and this is the thanks I get! At
> first I really cared about him with real sweet, tender feelings. I
> sure learned to close *that* side of me down. Caring wasn't worth
> it anymore. He was using me as his punching bag all the time.
> He's totally pitiful, and I feel sorry for him. I can't even really
> hold it against him. He's just screwed up.

For some of the African American battered women, this sense
of tolerance and forgiveness that Beverly's story illustrated caused
them to become detached from their previously lively lives. The
African American battered women typically sacrificed their desires, denied their feelings, and withdrew from aspects of their
lives that gave them pleasure, including making optimistic plans
for the future. In a sense, they began to give up on their lives.
They felt confused and disoriented. Some displaced their emotions onto their employers or members of their families of origin.

Renee, a twenty–seven–year–old African American woman
who was detained on an arson charge, was battered for six years
by her boyfriend. She said:

> Being abused by my man taught me that no matter what I may
> have thought about myself when I was growing up, I am really a
> piece of shit. The way I see it, it was a cruel joke that my family
> played on me. How could they let me think that I really had a
> chance in this world? When I got hip to the truth, I got real an-

gry at the world. I started doing the bad things that led me here. Why shouldn't I steal when I wanted something if that was the only way to get it? My motto became, "A worthless person can do worthless things, and it won't matter so much." How's that for a way to live!

In contrast, the white battered women's initial emotional responses and conceptualizations of the abuse were almost opposite. Typically, they were less likely to rationalize or deny the seriousness of the abuse, and they recognized the pattern of abuse for what it was much more quickly than the African American battered women did. They did not seem to engage in as much self–evaluation or analysis of external causes of the early abusive episodes, and, given that they were already isolated, they did not go through a process of social withdrawal. Their stories illustrated that they were less disappointed because they were less satisfied initially and had lower expectations.

Linda, a thirty–three–year–old white woman detained on a drug charge, was battered by her common–law husband for nine years. She said:

> I was a real typical battered woman from the time we got together. He was in control of everything: money, sex, our friends, how our house looked. Even though most men are like that, he was worse than how most men are. And do you know why he beat me? Because he was a crazy brute, not a man. He got some kind of sick pleasure out of hurting me with his hands *and* his words. I think he felt sorry at times, but he never apologized for his meanness. I realized early on that I couldn't really change him. What woman could ever change a man? What did I expect anyway? I only got together with him in the first place because I thought I was supposed to. He really never cared about me—no one did. I barely cared about myself! But I decided I'd better get out of this mess. I did things like took the pill behind his back so I wouldn't get pregnant. I started selling drugs to make money for an apartment, and I told everyone that if I was found dead it was because he had killed me. I don't really think that he would, but it was my way to let people know that I was in real trouble.

"I Just Couldn't Seem to Win."

A third characteristic of the African American battered women's experiences that contributed to their increasing vulnerability to abuse was a sense of shame and inadequacy that emerged when they first realized that the abuse symbolized their failure to accomplish their romantic dreams in their intimate relationships, much as they had failed in the public sphere. The women in this subgroup became involved with the men who later abused them when they were relatively young. Having had the privilege of extra attention and resources, they recalled believing that as they were growing up, their dreams (as influenced by dominant ideology) were within their reach. They had planned to establish a hegemonic, traditional, nuclear family. Even as they began to feel disenfranchised in the public sphere, the women recalled feeling like the one arena in which they *could* exercise power was the private sphere, as they had done as children. When they realized that their domestic power was being limited by the abuse, the African American battered women responded by working harder to establish a sense of order and control over their households, as opposed to deciding to leave them.

Their desperate attempts to make their violent marriages "work," lest their identities be *completely* shattered, led to profoundly immobilizing feelings of failure and self–blame, which resulted in increased vulnerability.

Inca, a thirty–one–year–old African American woman detained on a burglary charge, was battered by her husband for seven years. She said:

> What was I to do? I was scared, ashamed, had tried everything I could think of. I lost twenty–five pounds, I moved with him, I learned what he wanted in bed, I spent time with his creepy friends. He got every single thing he asked for from me. I was constantly running around him, trying to make the world a good place for him. Hell, it was an awful place for me too! But I still was more worried for him than myself. I even got him a job. And what did I get? I got beaten for trying to control his life, stabbed for trying to steal his friends, teased for showing off how much money I had when I bought him clothes, raped for having sex with other men. And then I would try to cool it, and I got beaten again for being "cold." I just couldn't seem to win. But did I stop trying? No!

Inca's statement illustrates the pattern of circumstances and emotional responses that lead to gender entrapment and abuse. Denial and rationalizations led to a sense of displaced self–blame as the women began to feel ashamed of their failure to create harmonious, protective family lives in keeping with the dominant ideology. At the same time, their childhood pattern of using their selves to enhance difficult situations and the few remaining optimistic aspects of their personalities led them to become even *more* vulnerable to abuse in their intimate relationships by trying harder. This pattern was a notable feature of gender entrapment for the African American battered women who attempted to stop, modify, and cope with the abuse instead of leaving the relationship. Typically, the violence escalated, they became more emotionally desperate, and the outside world became increasingly judgmental and suspicious of the African American battered women who would not reach out to protect themselves and and/or their children.

In contrast, the white battered women blamed themselves less and came to a more realistic awareness of the danger in their relationships sooner than the African American battered women did. Since their relationships were more likely to be violent from the beginning, and because they felt more inadequate in general, the white battered women had a more immediate sense of themselves as emotionally and socially vulnerable to abuse and mistreatment from their male partners. The white battered women in this study were not conflicted by a sense of failure to meet the ideological norm because, with the exception of the violence, their lives mirrored that norm. They did not internalize responsibility for their failed relationships to the same extent that the African American women did, for they did not have the expectation that it was possible for them to have happy, mutual adult relationships with men. With one exception, the white battered women denied feeling sorry for the men who abused them.

The exception was Clara, a forty–five–year–old white woman detained on a felonious drug charge who was battered for eighteen years by her African American husband. Clara said:

> I got involved with this man as a way to have a place to live, having run away from the foster home because of physical and emotional abuse from the men there. I took a bus to New York City and was hanging around Port Authority. I was seventeen

and he was much older than I was. When we met he was convinced that I was a hooker, which I wasn't at the time. This set
me up for lots of emotional abuse and sexual insults. All I
wanted was intimacy and a place to call home.... I was still
looking for a family. We were together for twenty–one years. He
could be really sweet or really awful. But, I admit, I thought he
was really cool because he was Black. His family was really
racist, and I thought this was a good way to get back at them.
Besides, the other girls I was hanging with were Black, and they
were the first people I knew who had any culture. I became very
dependent on him, and he basically was the one who took
charge of everything. The physical abuse began in the third year
of our relationship and got progressively worse. I was dragged by
the hair, locked in the house; he decided what I would wear and
whom I would see. He used to tell me, "I got you off the street,
so I can treat you like I want to." It got pretty bad after a while.
But, as a white girl, I couldn't rat on him. He had a job that supported us, and I sure didn't want him to lose it. I also learned
from the girls I used to hang with that it was really wrong to call
the police on a Black guy because of how they were treated. We
were living in Harlem, and I had seen what they did when they
arrested Blacks. So what could I do? I felt like, as a white, I had
to be really careful, just like the Black girls did.

Chris, a twenty–four–year-old white woman detained on an
assault charge, was battered by her husband for eight years. Her
story was more typical of the white women's responses. She said
this:

Hell no, I didn't feel sorry for him. He was a true monster,
bully, son of a bitch. He did whatever he wanted and, like every
other man I've ever known, he was arrogant and nasty. I should
have known.... Well, I sure found out quickly! It may have been
my fault for marrying him in the first place, but he's the one to
blame for my loss of hearing, my headaches, and my emotional
breakdown. I'm not any more sad or depressed than I ever was.
I'm just facing reality: men are scum, but since they have all of
the power, they can do whatever they want to do.

In sum, the comparison of the relational circumstances and
the emotional responses of the African American battered wom-

en and the white battered women in the early stages of abuse in their intimate relationships indicated how the white women's sense of vulnerability actually *protected* them from gender entrapment. Whereas the African American battered women were less realistic, more tolerant, and conciliatory and conscious of the pressures on their male partners from the social world, the white women were less so. The white battered women did the physical work of caring for their families and their households, but they did less emotional work on their male partners' behalf, in part because the white men had fewer negative events in the public sphere that would have required support from the women in their lives.

The African American non–battered women's relationships were different from both subgroups who experienced abuse from their male partners. First, they typically did not form monogamous, future–oriented relationships with men as early in their lives. Instead, their sexual and romantic partners changed more rapidly and they did not establish households with the men with whom they were involved. The African American non–battered women tended to have more peerlike or social relationships with men, and their young adult lives were not organized toward the goal of creating nuclear, heterosexual families. They were not uninterested in men, but rather they did not expect personal fulfillment, as the African American battered women did, or social fulfillment, as the white battered women did, from their intimate relationships. As such, the African American non–battered women were not vulnerable to gender entrapment.

It is important to note, however, that each of the five African American non–battered women in this study had experienced at least one episode of violence from men. Unlike the other two subgroups, though, the violence was typically not part of an intimate, long–term domestic relationship, and if it was, the African American non–battered women were less emotionally and symbolically attached to the relationship Karen, a twenty–year–old African American woman detained on a prostitution charge, said:

> Sure I've been hit. Who hasn't? I got into fights all the time
> with the brothers [African American men] I hang out with, but I
> never let a man beat me up. Hell no! And they will if you let

them, that's for sure. I know lots of them who slap their old
ladies [female partners] around, and they are real strong so they
hurt them too. That's why I will never let a man live in my
house. I have to have somewhere to send him when he starts to
act stupid. I grew up with crazy men, and I learned that it's better to be with them from a distance than live with them. I like
it like that. I go to my man when I want to, but my home is
mine. I'd live with a sister [an African American woman] any
day before I'd let a brother move in with me no matter what he
promises. And as far as being a battered woman goes, I will just
keep my distance, 'cause you don't know when any man might
go off on you for no reason. There is nothing any woman can do
to stop them... except have a way out. That's what I always try
to do, have a way out.

From this and other accounts from the African American
non–battered women, it can be seen how they were less vulnerable, in part, because of the circumstantial and emotional factors
in their adult households that resulted from a different gender–
identity development and relational expectations that were created in their households of origin. They had very different senses
of themselves, desired different types of relationships with men,
and had less invested in creating ideologically defined households. Two of the African American non–battered women had
been in long–term intimate relationships with women.

When the African American non–battered women were assaulted by their husbands or boyfriends, they responded very dif-
ferently from the women in the other two subgroups because
they were not as symbolicaly or emotionally attached to the relationships. Anita, a thirty–five–year–old African American
woman who was arrested on a drug charge recounted the following story:

I was beaten bad by this boyfriend I had once. I wasn't surprised;
he beat his other women before me. But I hit him back immediately, pulled out my piece [gun] and left the party right away.
When I moved in with my mother the next day, she told me that
she thought that man was no good anyway, and that I could
crash at her place for awhile. There was no room for me, but I
knew that I wasn't going back to that fool ever again. I'll face
my danger on the streets, but not at home. He knew better than

to come after me again.

Anita experienced one other episode of domestic assault, was raped by a stranger, and was regularly harassed by men on the street. While her life was by no means safe or comfortable, given the dangerous environment she lived in, she did not experience the type of ongoing, insidious domestic violence that characterizes gender entrapment. She described the incidents as fights that were more mutual in nature; she had more social support, and she did not have as much at stake in the relationship. The African American non–battered women were distinguished from the other group of African American women in particular by less loyalty to African American men and less interest in and ability to take care of men. They did not grow up with a sense of relative privilege that made them feel that they could change or control men's behavior.

This finding is important because it distinguishes the potential risk that all women face of male violence from the type of *ongoing abuse* that battered women experience and that characterizes the gender–entrapment theoretical model. Most of the women in this study, including the non–battered African American women, lived with the threat of violence every day. While this is not a study of abusive men per se, it can be inferred that the differences in these women's experiences of male violence were *not* solely their intimate male partners' inclination to use violence (since, statistically, at least twenty–five percent of all men regardless of racial/ethnic group or socioeconomic status are so inclined). Rather, this finding suggests that the variations between the subgroups are related to the dynamics between 1) gender–identity development; 2) early relational circumstances; 3) cultural loyalty to men; 4) women's response to male violence; and 5) social conditions. All of these factors, and the relationship between them, affect the consequences for women who are battered, and are incorporated into the gender–entrapment theoretical model of African American women's participation in illegal activities.

THE CONSEQUENCES OF MALE VIOLENCE

The previous discussion links the women's gender–identity development to the circumstantial and emotional factors that created some women's vulnerability to violence from their intimate partners. The pattern of violence, which included physical attacks, emotional abuse, and, for some women, sexual assaults, turned the women's domestic sphere into a situation of terror. This situation, which was created and controlled by the violent men, had significant long–term consequences that varied by subgroup of abused women.

"I lost my pride, my hope, and my fingers."

The Conflict Tactics Scale was administered to each of the thirty–seven women in the study to determine if they fit the operational definition of a "battered woman" set forth in the research design. The CTS score was also used to measure the extent of the physical violence in the abused women's relationships, and to compare the population interviewed in this study to other national samples. The results of the CTS confirmed that all but six of the thirty–two African American women in this study were battered, and all five of the white women experienced violence in their intimate relationships. The average CTS score of the twenty–six African American battered women was considerably higher than the national average. While this finding indicated the extreme nature of the abuse in a quantifiable way, a deeper appreciation of the women's experiences emerges through their descriptions in their own words of the insidious and profound nature of the abuse in their intimate relationships.

Juanita, a twenty–six–year–old African American women detained as a co–defendant on a homicide charge, was battered by her common–law husband for three years. She said:

> I was with a man for three years until I was arrested. He's a cruel, sick, mean man who tortured me, doing any and everything he could to keep my body and heart in pain. He beat me bad: hit me in the eye, cut me with a blade, made me stand on the hot plate that I used for cooking and slowly turned it up so my feet would burn up. You can't imagine the pain. My feet are ruined. The other thing he used to do was try to throw me out the window. He would tie me up and drag me over to the window laughing. Then he'd lean me out really far. I felt like I was going to fall the six stories to the ground. My ribs still hurt from leaning out. The next thing I knew he was pulling me back in, slugging me, kicking me, and twisting my arm behind my back. But the burning of my feet on the hot plate was the worst.

As Juanita's story illustrates, most of the African American women who were battered described heinous abuse that was extreme both in nature and extent. The violent assaults were characteristically routine, following a distinct temporal and sequential pattern, and they tended to escalate over time. Typically, the women in this subgroup were physically much weaker than their batterers, and they were very seriously hurt. The men used bodily force, weapons such as guns and knives, and household objects such as telephone wire, matches, or irons. For some women the violent episodes lasted for hours or even days.

Inca, a thirty–one–year–old African American woman detained for burglary and possession of stolen property, was abused by her husband for seven years. She said:

> When I got it, I got it good. He would start out by staring at me, and then he'd follow me around the apartment. The breaking of dishes was my sign that I was next. He'd shove me, and I would land up on the floor where he'd use a broken bottle, dish, or kitchen knife to scratch me, lightly at first and then harder. He was very strong and used his weight to hold me down. If I'd try to resist, he'd use a belt to tie me to the bed, the couch or the oven door. Then he'd start the real abuse... the hitting, kicking, the punching, slapping and all the rest. After he'd lock me in the closet or bedroom. I'd just sit there in pain wondering when he'd come at me again.

From the battered women's perspective, the permanent injury and disfigurement that resulted from the abuse was particularly significant. It included facial scars, loss of fingers, blindness, baldness, and burn marks. The disfigurement served as constant reminders of their suffering, and it created public humiliation. Many of the women said that when they were asked about the cause of their disability, they felt compelled to disclose details of their abusive relationship, and that people found it "unbelievable." The public manifestation of this disreputable private event had important implications for gender entrapment. The shame and loss of dignity that accompanied the disfigurement was significant; the African American battered women's sense of failure to accomplish their goal of creating an "ideal family" was permanently embedded in their consciousness through the obvious, long–term injury.

Karen, a twenty–year–old African American woman detained for prostitution, was battered by her common–law husband for three years. She said:

> We were together for five years. It was a nightmare by the time he was arrested. The abuse got so bad I lost my mind. And that's not all; I lost my pride, my hope, *and* my fingers. See this hand? I lost these fingers one night when he went real crazy. We'd been out at a party, and I was talking to this guy. He started on me right away. I was just having fun, but I knew I was in trouble by the look in his eye. He suddenly went and grabbed me, and we left. All the way home, he was holding my hand too tight and yelling at me. After a real good beating in the head, back and neck, I was starting to pass out. That really made him mad, and so he took the meat cleaver and chopped it down on my hand. I passed out completely then, and woke up in my bed with a towel around my bleeding hand. I'll never forget the pain or that crazy look of pleasure he used to get in his eye. This hand reminds me every single day that I can't use it on account of how he treated me. One part of my life is ruined forever. I'll never have it back. How do I explain that to my kids? They ask, just like everyone else. If I tell the truth, they think *I'm* the crazy one. If I don't, he still keeps me in his power.

A related set of issues for many of the African American battered women was chronic physical pain, drug and alcohol addiction, miscarriages, and long–term emotional disorders that were a consequence of being abused. More than half of the African American women who were battered were prevented by their abusive partners from seeking medical attention for injuries they caused during an assault, and some women "medicated" themselves with drugs or alcohol—typically supplied by their batterers. Twelve of the African American battered women associated the onset of abuse with their first pregnancy, which is consistent with the literature on battering.

Juanita, a thirty–six–year–old African American detained on a felonious drug charge, had been beaten for the last nine years of her twelve years of marriage. She said:

> Spanking was his thing. They started when I got pregnant. He thought I was pregnant by someone he introduced me to when

we were getting high. It was impossible, but he was just so jealous. He would follow me and jump me when I was walking down the street, and knock me down. I never had any time alone, and he wouldn't let me go to my mother's house any-more...not that she wanted anything to do with me since I started using [drugs]. He tried to tell me the spankings were for my good, to get me to stop using drugs so the baby wouldn't get hurt. What he didn't know that being beaten up was just one more excuse to get high. The worst was when he started punching me in the stomach or kicking my breasts. *That's* why I lost the baby, not because of the drugs.

From years of being severely assaulted on a regular basis, some of the women complained of chronic headaches, backaches, or limited range of motion in their limbs, as Lila's story illustrated. She was a thirty–two–year–old African American woman who was battered for eleven years by her husband. While being detained on a burglary charge, she said:

I've been hit, stabbed, had bones broken...all of that. He would come home at night when I was asleep, and I would wake up with a gun pointed to my head just because he was hungry or with a knife at my back because I was moaning in my sleep and he wanted to know who I was dreaming about. I was afraid to say anything....It was hard to tell what would tip him off. I started drinking to numb the pain. I was braver, slept better, and I could raise my arms to braid my daughter's hair when I was drunk. Sober, I was just a bunch of nerves. When he put my back out, I thought I was going to die from the pain. Even now, I can't stand or sit for too long. Since I've been sober, I can only raise my arms half way.

The life–history interviews with white battered women revealed that compared to the African American battered women, they typically experienced less severe physical abuse. Their CTS scores were closer to the national average, and, while they too were seriously hurt, their descriptive accounts of the nature and extent of abuse were less extreme than the African American battered women. The assaults were frequent and routine, but they did not escalate with the same speed. Most significantly, the abusive episodes were less degrading and humiliating in nature than what the African American women described.

Clara, a forty–five–year-old white women detained on a drug charge, was married to the man who abused her for twenty–one years. She said:

> It was hard to be beat by a man who you loved for twenty–one years. I knew he was kind of off when I met him, but I didn't ever think he would use his body against me. He was very strong, and would punch me, slap me, and shove me around the house. He never used a weapon against me, and he knew when to stop. It was as if he really let himself, he would kill me, and he didn't want to go to jail....and now look at who is here! I guess he knew just what he was doing...what the limits were and how to stay just enough inside of them to not hurt me so bad that I'd ever really have a case against him. The only scars are places no one would see. He even cut himself just to make it look like the fighting was equal. Now that I think of it, it is what really makes me feel stupid. He outsmarted me over and over!

"The Worst Thing Was the Shame."

Both the African American battered women and the white battered women described the emotional abuse as particularly painful, compounding their vulnerability to violence in their intimate relationships. Whereas the physical abuse led to pain, fear and, for some women, embarrassment, the emotional abuse created a sense of powerlessness, inadequacy, and alienation for most of the women who were battered. The *combined* effect of being insulted, discredited, and teased, *and* being beaten up was a deadly one—some women came to feel that they *deserved* to be battered (sometimes the women referred to the violent episodes as being "punished") for being "poor," "bad mothers," "ugly," "stupid," or "sluts." Typically, as the emotional abuse escalated, the battered women became less likely to defend themselves or to reach out for help, becoming more isolated and, therefore, much more vulnerable. As the research on domestic violence indicates, it is indeed the emotional wearing down of a woman's hope and self-worth that is a major factor in a man's ability to maintain dominance and control over a battered woman, once fear and injury is established through physical violence. This *combination* of emotional and physical abuse, and the fact that women are at significant risk even if they leave the relationship, help to explain why some women stay in violent and abusive circumstances.

For the African American women who were battered, the effects of emotional abuse and private humiliation factored into gender entrapment in a particularly profound way. In addition to the ongoing degradation described above, six women reported being made to beg for food, and one was forced to eat human feces. Two of the African American battered women reported being locked out of their apartments all night nude or semi–nude. Eight were routinely locked in rooms or closets. Four were denied sleep for days at a time, and three reported that they were restrained and forced to consume alcohol until they became physically ill.

Renee, a twenty–seven–year–old African American woman detained on an arson charge, was abused by her boyfriend for six years. She said:

> The abuse started slowly, and at first I felt like he was just moody. I would soothe him any way I could, and he seemed to respond. Those days people still thought that I was lucky to have him, and I never told how badly he really treated me. I would clean up from his rages, put makeup on my bruises, and make up stupid excuses for the injuries he caused. Usually, I was really strong about it. But when I would break down and cry, which wasn't very often, he would take me into the bathroom and push my head under the water in the toilet. He'd act like he was going to flush it, but I don't remember that he ever did. But what made it worse was that he would then tell his friends about it... calling me "toilet head" and "shit–eater." Once he really made me eat shit right in front of our children at the table. I thought I was just going to die. Who would ever have imagined that this man would be able to make me to stoop so very low! Being hit... well, that hurt. Being made to feel like a fool—that almost killed me.

In most cases, the emotional abuse served to disorient the African American battered women, for in addition to making them afraid of the batterer (whom they had thought they could love and trust), the emotional abuse decreased the level of confidence that was created by their privileged positions in their families of origin. Therefore, being humiliated in front of their children and other family members was a particularly painful and insidious aspect of abuse.

Sebina, a thirty–two–year-old African American woman detained on a murder charge, was married to a man who abused her for four years. She said:

> For me the worse thing was the shame I brought to my family. Here I was, the prize child, working in a good job with two lovely children. I was very happy and successful, and I still had the admiration and respect of my family. They loved to come to my house and see how well I was doing. My family didn't know, at first, that this man was such a tyrant. They knew that he had some problems keeping a job and that he was not very responsible around the children; however, they felt like since he had been with me he was doing much better....If anyone could turn Keith around, Sebina could!" I believed that too, but it just wasn't working out so well. He was battering me pretty badly, using his fist and anything else he could find to hit me with: punching me in the face, hitting me all over my body with lamps, banging my head against the table...stuff like that. I couldn't seem to work my charm the way I usually could. Deep down inside I thought there was something wrong with me or I'd be able to stop this abuse. I was starting feeling like a complete failure since I couldn't get it together even with all the extras I was given in life. The day he threw me across the room at my parents' house was the worst. I got all caught up in protecting him from them, protecting them from him, trying to get the kids to go into the yard. I thought I was going to die from the humiliation, not the abuse! Suddenly, I couldn't keep a job, I stopped taking an interest in my kids, and church didn't mean as much to me. It was like I was wilting under the pressure to keep up a front and the put–downs were working to make me feel like shit.

As Sebina's story indicates, the abuse had a *particular* significance for gender entrapment for those African American women who had a relatively privileged status in their households of origins. These women described how their self–esteem plummeted as a result of the emotional abuse and physical assaults. The simultaneous lack of success in the public world that some of the

African American battered women began to experience reinforced their newly acquired sense of shame, failure, and vulnerability in their private relationships.

The white battered women in this study also experienced
emotional abuse as a traumatic and complicating factor in their
violent relationships. Their experiences were distinguished from
the African American battered women in several ways. First, because the white battered women tended to be more isolated from
the onset of the relationships, the emotional abuse created a
more immediate, private suffering, and yet they recovered from
it more rapidly.

Gwen, a thirty–three–year–old white woman detained on an
aggravated sexual assault and sodomy charges, was abused by her
husband for seven years. She said:

> This man had a sick kind of control over me. As soon as I met
> him, I felt my small world getting smaller. I was losing the few
> friends I had, and it was as if he was controlling every side of my
> life. When the abuse started—actually it was before I was mar-
> ried—he kept me inside, watched my every move, and never let
> me out of his sight. Of course there was nowhere I could go any-
> way since I left family to be with him, and they lost interest in
> me like that. I was his punching bag. He broke my nose twice,
> and I lost count of the black eyes he gave me. But what was
> worse was the yelling, the laughing at me when I cried, and the
> nasty things he'd say to me. To keep me inside he would cut up
> my clothes. When I cooked, he would make me feed the chil-
> dren first to prove I wasn't poisoning him. If I gave the children a
> bath, he would rush in and hassle me, saying that I was touching
> them nasty, when actually it was him that was doing that. But I
> just couldn't win with him. So I just gave up trying. It was less
> trying on me that way, and I felt relief.

The white battered women blamed themselves for the abuse to
a lesser extent than did the African American battered women.
As they told their stories, they seemed to have been less confused by the violence; it was not as inconsistent with their expectations and experiences of relationships between women and
men. They understood that the physical abuse was a sign to get
help, and, as such, the emotional abuse did not claim as much
power over their thoughts about themselves, the decisions they

made, their identities, or their relationships within their families. Gwen continued:

> I knew as soon as the hitting started that I was in a heap of trouble. He was the devil—beating me silly every day almost. It got so I was almost used to it. I thought he was going to kill me if I didn't do something. Even though it took me a long time to figure out what to do about it. I knew that eventually I would have to do something. I'd seen it too many times before, and I knew in my heart that it would be over one day. I knew that he'd never leave, so that I'd just have to figure out a way to get the hell out of this marriage. I decided that I'd get away as soon as my kids were grown.

Ironically, because the white battered women did not have the inflated sense of power or self–confidence that the African American women had, their self–esteem and expectations for the future were not barriers to their reaching out for help when they really needed it. While the white battered women's responses demonstrated some degree of denial, they did not seem to be as profoundly immobilized by the abuse as the African American battered women were. So while the white men were not less emotionally abusive per se, the emotional abuse had a different meaning for the white women, which differentiates their experiences from the gender entrapment that characterized the experiences of the African American battered women whose stories are told in this book.

> "I have three of my four kids because
> he raped me."

The amount and nature of sexual abuse, including marital rape, emerged as perhaps the most insidious and traumatic aspect of the abuse for both the African American battered women and the white battered women. Certainly the sexual abuse was the aspect of their relationships that was the most difficult for the women to talk about during the life–history interviews. For the most part, the findings about sexual abuse did not vary significantly by race/ethnicity. All of the white women and seventeen of the twenty–six African American women who were battered reported marital rape. The pattern that emerged in both populations indicated that typically these women were sexually abused soon after the physical assaults, when the women were hurt, bruised, bleeding, and emotionally distraught. The sexual abuse included forced intercourse, rape using objects like hairbrushes or broomsticks, and being forced to perform degrading sexual acts while viewing pornographic material. The women I interviewed reported a range of psychological consequences that characterize sexual abuse, including a detachment from their bodies, subsequent self–neglect or self–abuse, and a sense of shame that deepened their isolation and stigma.

Letisha, a thirty–seven–year–old African American women detained on a forgery charge, who was abused for thirteen years by her husband, said:

> As a Black woman, there is nothing more awful than being used by my man for sex. Such disrespect! It is like they say women were treated on the plantation: to have our bodies used and abused, to have our hearts broken, and *then* to be forced into sex with the very person who stole our dignity. Of all the things that I couldn't stand, having him all over me after beating me up was the worst. It made me feel like I was a true "nigger," and he, of all people, was my master.

Linda, a thirty–three–year-old white woman detained on a felonious drug charge, was abused by her husband of nine years. She said:

> The sexual part of our relationship was the most tense. It was the way he hurt me the worst. Right after he'd attack me and threaten me with one of his guns, he would start in on my body, telling me that I was too messy and too smelly to have sex with him. He would send me to the shower, and then he would follow me, throw me on the bathroom floor and rape me, including putting himself in my butt, then in my mouth. It was awful, and it hurt. I was really starting to go crazy. After he broke my ribs, he stopped the bathroom routine... but the rapes continued in the bedroom.

For some of the African American and the white battered women, a sexual assault was the final violent act of *each* abusive episode. Ironically, in this way, being raped came to symbolize relief. For others, as the following case illustrated, a sexual encounter was the only way the women felt they could avoid a violent episode: a cruel, ironic twist on the meaning of sexuality in their intimate relationships, as Jeanne, a thirty–three–year–old African American women charged with robbery, described. She was battered by her boyfriend for seven years. She said:

> No, he didn't really rape me, but I remember feeling like when he was getting tense that the best way to avoid being hit was to seduce him into bed with me. That way, he could put his bad energy into sex rather than abuse. Sure it hurt sometimes, but the pain was not as bad as when he'd whip my ass. Seducing him still makes me feel ashamed of myself. I never had an honest desire for sex with him after I started doing this. In fact, I don't think I'll ever have a desire for anyone again. I can't seem to think about sex without the fear. It's slimy and makes me feel like a real slut.

In addition to the immediate physical and emotional consequences of marital rape, most of the women like Jeanne described the long–term impact of sexual abuse by their adult male partners. Several of the women who were forced to be sexual either immediately after or during an assault felt at the time of the interview as if they would never be able to experience the enjoyment of an intimate sexual relationship again. Some who became pregnant as a result of being raped felt as if their relationships with their children would always be tainted by the violence, which had led two to surrender custody of their children to child protective services.

Selma, a thirty–year–old African American woman detained on a murder charge, was battered for six years by her husband. She said:

> I have three of my four kids because he raped me. He's used his gun, the plunger, or anything he could get his dirty hands on. Sometimes he used himself.... Funny, that was the worst. I was either pregnant, miscarrying, or having babies all the time. Even when the physical abuse would let up, he would keep this nonsense up. Now that I am in here (at Rikers), I don't really even want to hear about or see my kids. They are only a reminder of the things he used to do to me. When he brings them to visit me, I know he is trying to hurt me. Because he knows how I feel. Even in the visit room he is always trying to feel me up.

On the impact of sexual abuse, there was some divergence between those battered women who had been sexually abused as children or raped by strangers, and those who had not. Generally the white battered women and the African American battered women felt that the sexual abuse from their husbands or boyfriends created a *particularly* painful loss of identity, confidence ,and self–esteem. It was extremely difficult for them to deal with the fact that their sense of themselves as sexual beings and wives was being "ruined" by constant forced sexual acts. Margaret, a twenty–one–year–old white woman detained on a harassment charge who was battered by her boyfriend for three years, said:

> As a woman you come to expect certain things from living on the streets or if you come from a home like I did. You couldn't ever tell who you'd meet, and you couldn't control your grandfather's roaming fingers up inside of you. But I never, ever imagined that I'd be raped by the man I chose to marry. For a while, I didn't even know it was rape. I thought it was my problem with sex or something from my past. All I knew was that it felt wrong, it hurt, and it made me feel really like the piece of ass the men who raped earlier told me I would become.

Of the nine African American women who were battered but *denied* that sexual abuse was part of their adult intimate relationships, a significant pattern emerged. This group typically felt that the sexual aspect of their relationships was, in fact, the best part of the relationships. All of these women I interviewed were involved with men who were substance abusers, and who used drugs and/or alcohol during their sexual encounters. This finding contradicted the current literature in the field of substance abuse that suggests that drug abuse heightens violence against women; indeed, for those women who were physically battered but not sexually abused by their intimate partners, drug and alcohol abuse during sex seemed to be the one thing that would successfully establish intimacy in their relationships.

Johnetta, a thirty–six–year–old African American woman detained on a drug abuse charge, was battered for nine years by her husband. She said:

> The one thing he didn't do was abuse me in bed. In fact, we had

very wild, hot sex. Looking back, sometimes it was rough, but at the time it was the only good part of our life. When we had sex when we were high together is when it was best for me because he was less strong, it was over faster, and he was more romantic. He'd really talk about his feelings and how he wanted us to be better and closer. That's one excuse I used for getting high—to have good sex.

THE WOMEN'S RESPONSE TO THE VIOLENCE

The African American battered women in the sample gradually became very isolated by the violence done to them. They stopped visiting their families, lost or changed jobs, stayed indoors more, and interrupted social and religious participation. The women told how their vulnerability to violence, and the severity of the physical, emotional, and sexual consequences influenced their behaviors and the concrete action they took in response.

Carolyn, a thirty–year–old African American woman detained on a homicide charge, was battered by her husband for twelve years. She said:

My family didn't know about the abuse in the beginning. They have told me since that they wondered why I stopped coming around so much, but they didn't really have time to worry about me. I used to wear long–sleeved blouses even in the summer, and I got real good at using foundation to cover up a black eye or two. I really did a great job. Once, though, my neighbors called the police, and when they came, he made me peek through a very small opening in the door and tell the police I was okay. That shows how really dumb the cops are. I was smiling through my tears, my hair was a mess, and the kids were screaming because they were so afraid. All the officers cared about was getting on with their coffee break. Just because I could smile, they left. As soon as they left, he started beating me again, and that's when I learned that it was better not having people involved because when they didn't help, all that did was to make him feel more powerful. He said, and I'll never forget this, "See, everyone knows that this is between you and me, and since you are mine, you'll do what I say."

The degree to which the women were able to "disappear"

without families, friends, or community groups questioning and/or objecting was significant. It is illustrative of their families' sense of the women's independence, the relatively fragile nature of their social networks, and the fact that their families were more concerned with relatives whose lives were more obviously in crisis.

As Juanita, a twenty–six–year–old African American battered woman detained on a homicide charge who was battered by her common–law husband for three years, said:

> I guess, for them, my problem was small. I'd always taken care of myself before, so why should they worry. Here's one brother in jail, the other strung out on drugs, my sister is pregnant again and she has AIDS, my mama is trying to keep a job when her hospital is laying people off.... What's a little abuse to them? At least I had a place to sleep. But what they didn't know was that I was passing out from the blows to my head. With them trying to hold it together—trying to keep folks alive and out of jail, how could I lay this on them? Go to counseling? Call the police? Come on, let's be real. I was not anywhere near the top of the list of people I knew who needed help. And since my family and friends always thought I could take care of myself, they never even thought that my problems would be so bad as they were. No, there was so much suffering around, everyone thought mine was lightweight.

As Juanita's story illustrates, the African American battered women were less likely than the white women to use social services, battered women's programs, or to go to the hospital. Some African American women recalled not feeling like the problem warranted outside intervention, that they could handle it by themselves. Others tried to reach out to services only to find out that they were categorically excluded because of their drug use or other circumstances. One African American battered woman who disclosed that she was sexually attracted to a woman, which was the excuse her boyfriend gave for beating her, was denied assistance from a religious–based program for battered women. Most felt, for one reason or another, that their experiences did not fall within the category deserving of services. Being a "battered woman" did not fit into their identities either because they fought back or because they felt that the men in their lives were *not* more powerful than they were.

Johnetta, a thirty–six–year–old African American woman detained on a drug charge, was battered by her husband for nine years. She said:

> Part of my problem is that I am a strong Black woman. I am angry, and some people think I am too loud. So even though he beat me almost to death, I beat him too. If I had been as strong as he was, we'd both be in trouble. But since I wasn't as strong, he got away with almost murdering me. It's as simple as that. The broken bones, the scar where he cut my face... all of those are because he was stronger outside, and I was stronger inside. By that I mean I'm no regular battered woman, because he got his share of licks. It wasn't until he started playing the mind games on me that I was really vulnerable to him. And how do you call the police and admit that he is making you crazy, making you drink, sticking the works (needles) in your arm? Don't forget, drugs are against the law.

Other reasons that the African American battered women reported not reaching out for help included a general mistrust of social services based on previous experiences, the batterers' control of their mobility and phone use, and their own involvement in criminal activities.

To understand gender entrapment it is important to note the avoidance of criminal justice intervention in particular. Kim, a thirty–seven–year–old African American woman arrested on a prostitution charge, who was battered by her husband for twelve years, said:

> Call the police? Never! Everyone I knew spent all of our time running from the police! The cops are the worst people to get involved in a family problem, probably because they beat up on women too! I know it because my girlfriend's old man is a cop, and he is an abuser himself. The station house is full of drug–using, prostitute–using, woman–hating men. *That's* why they are called pigs. Seriously though, I just never could really trust that they would help me and not just use my 911 call as one more excuse to beat up a Black man. They were never that decent to me or anyone I knew. I just couldn't do it. I learned early in my life that the cops were dangerous to my people. They were to be avoided at all costs.

Not using police or other public services was a conscious decision that most of the African American battered women made. For them, that decision was consistent with the extent of police brutality that existed in their cities and with their loyalty to their community—particularly the men in it. Seeing social services—especially the police—as the opposition created more isolation, vulnerability and, ultimately, public scrutiny of the African American battered women. This is a central aspect of gender entrapment.

Janet, a forty–six–year–old African American battered woman who was battered for ten years and detained on a homicide charge, said:

> When I finally went for help they asked why I waited so long. There was no police record, no counselor to testify, and no family witness. I could tell that the judge didn't believe me, especially because he went on and on about how I "seemed so smart and all." Now what's that supposed to mean? That he's dumb? I don't want any white judge talking about my man that way. Or did he mean that the sisters (African American women) are dumb? Either way, it was a put–down that I didn't appreciate at all. So to answer him, *that's* why I didn't go for help sooner.

The white battered women were typically more isolated from the beginning of their relationships than the African American battered women were. As such, the violence did not *create* isolation, as it did for the African American battered women. Rather the isolation and dependency created their *vulnerability* to men's violence. With her face still swollen from the broken jaw, and with two of her teeth missing, Linda, a thirty–three–year–old white woman detained on a drug possession charge, said:

> I really think it would have been different if I had some outlets. All I had was him, and he was so bad to me. If I had someone to talk to or to notice, it would have helped me sooner. But, being the loner in the world that I am, I had no one to help me. Actually, I had to have my jaw broken and my two front teeth punched out before anyone would believe me that I was battered. Of course, I answered yes, and that was the beginning of the end. She gave me some phone numbers, and I was just getting ready to call when I got arrested for drugs. Oh, well, at least I am safe from him here.

The women in this subgroup tended to tell more people about the abuse, to reach out for emergency assistance, and not to be as concerned with concealing the signs of abuse as the African American battered women were. They identified as "battered women" and sought out the services that were available. In particular, the white battered women were much more likely than the African American battered women to use criminal justice agencies or other public services, although they were not necessarily any more likely to get an effective response.

Margaret was a twenty–seven–year–old white women detained on a harassment charge. She was battered for three years by her husband. She said:

> Calling the police was a routine event in my house. Eventually even the kids learned to call, but it never really helped. They would come, eventually, but I could tell that they were afraid to come into my building. They would stay downstairs and ask my husband to come down. Can you believe it? It was that typical "Come on, pal, let's take a walk around the block so you can cool off" routine. Like they really understood why my husband would batter me, and like I had no needs or opinions. Oh yes, I tried to get help a lot of times, but I guess my problems just weren't important enough to anyone but me and my kids.

CONCLUSION

By comparing the two subgroups of battered women in the study, important features of gender entrapment are illuminated. The African American battered women entered into their intimate relationships with optimism that resulted from their heightened status in their households of origin. As their experiences in the public sphere were disappointing, they became more strongly committed to establishing a respectable and successful domestic life, which, for them, included arranging their lives in accordance with the dominant ideology about gender roles in nuclear families. This desire and their efforts toward this goal posed a particular challenge for them; their African American male partners were excluded from opportunities that characteristically lead to male privilege (like earning more money than women), and the African American battered women themselves felt forced to participate actively in the public domains.

Feeling sorry for the men they were involved with, the women denied their vulnerability and tolerated the abuse, which, in turn, became worse while the women disbelieved that they were being hurt and humiliated by the men for whom they were caring. When they realized that their domestic lives were failing them, they isolated themselves out of shame and embarrassment and in order to protect the image of their family. The African American battered women were, therefore, increasingly vulnerable to the abuse and domination of their violent male partners.

The circumstantial and emotional factors that characterized the white battered women's adult households were different. They entered their intimate relationships with lower self–esteem and fewer expectations. That their relationships were unsatisfying and, indeed, abusive from the onset did not surprise or confuse them. Their identity was not as damaged by the abuse, and they did not become as immobilized as the African American battered women. When they were hurt, afraid, and humiliated, they planned to or attempted to get help. Even when their attempts were unsuccessful, they *felt* less trapped by the abuse and by their feelings about the men with whom they were involved.

These differences in vulnerability led to different consequences for the African American and the white women who were battered. First, the effects of the abuse varied considerably in terms of race/ethnicity. The variation was not related to the presence or absence of abuse per se, but rather the women's stories indicated that the meanings the abuse had for the women was different for each subgroup. The CTS scores and the women's personal accounts indicated that the African American women suffered particularly degrading forms of physical abuse from their male partners while the white battered women's CTS scores and accompanying accounts of abuse were more consistent with the national average; the abuse was of a more controlled nature. An important difference between the two subgroups on this item was the degree to which the African American battered women were permanently disfigured and suffered chronic pain from the physical abuse. This overt, public manifestation of being abused had a profoundly effective role in the gender–entrapment process—it furthered the African American women's deep loss of dignity, given their previously heightened sense of themselves.

In terms of emotional abuse, the women I interviewed in both subgroups described the horrific, damaging effect of regular psychological victimization. When combined with physical assaults, both groups of battered women were made further vulnerable by the damage caused by the insulting, dishonest, controlling behavior of their male partners. Women from each group described how the isolation, shame, loss of dignity and the fear created an interlocking pattern of vulnerability and violence that kept many women immobilized in the abusive relationships. The African American battered women experienced this pattern as far more disorienting than did the white battered women, most of whom were quicker to recognize it as abusive. In some ways the white battered women were more pessimistic and were emotionally hurt earlier in their lives, and, therefore they were less affected by the emotional abuse of their adult intimate partners. Furthermore, the social and familial stigma that the African American battered women anticipated or experienced was a complicating factor for them, given their privileged status in their households of origin and family–loyalty issues. In contrast, the white battered women were more estranged from their families of origin. In this way, the emotional abuse had a more powerful effect on the African American battered women than the white women in this sample and, as such, indicated a particular aspect of the gender entrapment theme.

In terms of those women who experienced sexual abuse, the life–history interviews revealed little difference between the two subgroups. Both the African American battered women and the white battered women found the marital rape and other forms of sexual violence extraordinarily difficult to bear, and they suffered long–term negative consequences. The effects were not affected by the presence or absence of sexual abuse as children.

The women's increased vulnerability to violence from their intimate partners and the consequence of the abuse affected their practical responses, influencing a distinct pattern of concrete behavior from the two groups of battered women in this study. The African American battered women's stories show how they attempted to conceal the abuse and avoided use of public services, while the white women tended to reach out to more individuals and to social–service programs. This finding is particularly noteworthy in terms of use of the criminal justice system for crisis–intervention services given that the women were, indeed, victims of a crime. Unlike most of the white women, the African American battered women had a distinct and vehement opposition to calling the police; they avoided pressing criminal charges against their abusive partners or otherwise becoming involved in a criminal justice solution to the violence. The extent to which mistreatment by law–enforcement officials, biased criminal justice practices, and the knowledge of the disproportionate incarceration rates of men of color consciously influenced the African American battered women's response to the abuse in their intimate relationships was significant. This intentional avoidance was obviously a very important finding for the study of the gender–entrapment theoretical model, and helps to explain how women were forced or lured into compromising, illegal activities.

5

SIX PATHS TO CRIME

"I was running, dealing, robbing, and stealing."

THIS CHAPTER describes the six paths that the
women whose stories are told in this book took to the illegal activities that resulted in their arrests as the final category of
events that constituted their gender entrapment. Drawing on the
findings from the previous two chapters, the discussion here em-
phasizes how the variations in gender–identity development led
to distinct types of vulnerability and abuse in intimate relationships that, for some women, compelled them to commit crimes.
The findings are again discussed by subgroup to highlight the
unique sets of circumstances that *race/ethnicity* and *intimate
violence* created for the women interviewed for this book.

It is important to note that the framework used in this chapter
to describe the women's experiences—the six paths to illegal activity—was not organized around legal definitions or official categories of crimes. Nor does the chapter focus on women's experiences once they were in the correctional system (see Chapter
One). Rather, as the study was designed to explore the link between gender identity, violence, and crime as a way to explain
some women's illegal behavior, the six paths serve here as a
framework for analysis of these particular women's experiences.
Therefore, the women's *own* versions of their charges, the fac-

tors that *they* believed influenced their arrests, and the details of their cases are presented from the women's points of view. These will then be organized into the six paths to illegal activities and presented here as conceptual categories that emerged from the data in order to explain the remaining aspects of the gender–entrapment theory.

It is also important to note that the coding of the findings into these six paths was a conceptual exercise consistent with the methodology described in Chapter Two of this book. It involved collapsing and renaming some illegal activities. So, for example, the crimes that the women in this sample were *arrested* for did not necessarily represent what they actually did. Furthermore, in many of their cases, there was considerable overlap in crimes—drug users may have been involved in illegal sex work and women arrested for theft may have also been charged with child abuse. The central and most important factor in the categorization process was how the *women who were interviewed* interpreted, reported, and ultimately understood their involvement in criminal activities and how the findings from the life-history interviews revealed six distinct paths to jail.

SUMMARY OF ANTECEDENT EVENTS

Prior to discussing the six paths that the women took to Rikers Island, the key issues that characterized each subgroup and influenced their involvement in illegal activities are reviewed. For the African American battered women, a central factor in the gender–entrapment explanation for their participation in illegal activities was the series of shifts in their identities. Their sense of being competent and desirable African American children, created by their positions in their households of origin, was first threatened by their limited social success as African American young women in the public sphere. They began to feel occupationally, educationally, or economically ineffective as their social options were limited. As they felt their social position becoming marginalized, their public identity became more fragile. Still, they continued to believe that "successful" family life was within their reach and held to their childhood dreams of ideologically defined relationships. Their longing for intimacy, respect, and a sense of accomplishment that they had been led to believe was possible in their home was heightened as they became more socially disenfranchised. The nature of the trauma associated with onset of violence in their intimate relationships effectively began to destroy their sense of themselves and their abilities to establish and maintain an ideologically "normal life" in an extraordinarily profound way. As the women were traumatized, threatened with constant emotional, physical, and sexual abuse, seriously injured, permanently disfigured, and fearful that the batterers would kill them, their identities were seriously shaken.

As their sense of themselves was shifting, the African American battered women began to feel betrayed and abandoned by their families and other helping institutions, having grown up with extended, albeit fragile, networks that they had expected would support them. Even though few reached out directly for emergency assistance, and most went to great lengths to conceal the abuse initially, as the abuse became more severe, they reported over and over again in the interviews, they felt as if *someone* should have helped them. While seemingly contradictory, these beliefs assumed a certain logic. It was as if the African American battered women's sense of entitlement—which had been buried deep below their loyalties to men, their commitment to ideology about family life, and their tolerance of the abuse in their intimate relationships—resurfaced, and they became genuinely frustrated at the lack of assistance from the police, health–care providers, and other helping agencies. So the African American battered women came to resent the isolation that they, in part, created. They were frustrated by their inability to change the situation because of the extreme nature of the violence or because of feeling loyalty, stigma, and lack of power in the public sphere. These women's resistance to turning to the criminal justice system in particular when they were battered and breaking the law cemented their gender entrapment.

In contrast, the precipitating circumstances that influenced the African American women who were not battered and their participation in illegal activities were dramatically different. These women grew up in more marginalized households that were not as rigidly organized around dominant ideology as the African American battered women's households. Their identities were less influenced by family expectations, pressure to please adults or to live up to a culturally constructed image of womanhood. As young children and as adult women, they saw the public sphere as an inhospitable, alienating environment, and they perceived people other than their peers—their parents, the police, social–service workers, health care providers—as their adversaries.

The African American women who were not battered were not surprised by their lack of social success when they entered the public sphere. Their limited educational attainment or occupational instability, for example, was consistent with their childhood images of adult life, and they did not grow up expecting to create a particular family form. So, as adults, they did not engage in activities to enhance the images of their domestic life or intimate relationships.

Obviously, the most significant difference between the African American battered women and the African American women who were not battered was that they were not regularly assaulted, fearful, degraded, or injured by their husbands or boyfriends. The non–battered African American women's paths to illegal activities were, therefore, influenced less by violence, the threat of violence, identity shifts, and the lack of social support. More often, they committed crimes because of drug use and addiction, poverty, peer relationships, and a sense of hopelessness that came to characterize their lives, which they perceived as being void of options for social success. As such, the gender–entrapment theory does not apply to their experiences.

The influential events for the white battered women rendered their experiences also inconsistent with the gender–entrapment theory. First and foremost, the women in this subgroup were less burdened by privileged status and loyalties to men than the African American battered women. On the contrary, the white women in this sample felt inferior and subordinate to the people around them. They had low self–esteem and felt personally ineffective from a very young age. Second, in contrast to the African American non–battered women, the white women did not perceive the world as a fundamentally hostile place that was organized in such a way as to limit their success. The white women came to interpret their lack of social success as the result of individual negative experiences or, for some, their own character flaws, rather than categorical alienation based on their race/ethnicity. They believed that the effects of being poor and victimized female children created their marginalized status and shaped their identities as adult women. Their identities did not shift as they were growing up in response to critical external events as the African American battered women's identities did.

Therefore, for the white battered women, being battered did not create a discrepancy between their expectations and their experiences. Their sense of themselves remained consistent with the identities that were constructed in their childhoods. So, for example, feelings of vulnerability to men's authority and powerlessness in the face of brutal violence were not unusual or new experiences for them, and consequently, the white women did not put as much effort into understanding, coping with, or changing their abusive relationships. Instead, they put energy into trying to leave their batterers. Like the African American battered women, they were frustrated and felt mistreated by unresponsive helping institutions; however, they did not report feeling betrayed, stigmatized, or confused. The white battered women's path to illegal activities were, therefore, influenced by fear and injury, like the African American battered women, and poverty, like the African American non–battered women, but were distinctly void of the loyalty–nihilism dialectic that emerged among the groups of African American women whose stories are told in this book.

These antecedent events and precipitating circumstances distinguish the three subgroups in this sample from each other and illustrate how the broader context of personal history, cultural values, dominant ideology, economic circumstance, and social location combined to create the gender entrapment that influenced the African American battered women's experiences along the path to illegal activities.

PATH I. WOMEN HELD HOSTAGE
"I knew he'd eventually kill one of us."

Perhaps the most heinous path to Rikers Island is represented by those women who were arrested for the death of one of their children. In this study, all four women detained on such charges were African American battered women who were abused by the men who killed their children. These women were arrested as co–defendants, conspirators, or on homicide charges and, if found guilty, would face sentences in state correctional facilities of eight years to life in prison. In some ways, these cases illustrated gender entrapment most vividly. They were the most severe cases of abuse; they had the highest CTS scores, the most insidious emotional abuse, and the most extreme isolation.

Sebina, a thirty–two–year–old African American woman, was arrested on a homicide charge in the death of her son. She married soon after her son was born. Battered by her husband for four years, she said:

> What happened was my co–defendant wanted me to stop caring for my boy, who was only four years old. He was jealous of him and tried to take over from me and be his father. At first I was glad because it made us seem more like a real family, but my son was very close to me. So when we would fight, he would cry and run to me, even when I tried to keep him back. Sometimes he got hurt by trying to cover me. My husband didn't know anything about raising kids, and I did. I kept trying to tell him that a child has to learn slowly. So like when I was trying to teach him letters, he would just scream at him and say, "You are a stupid boy," and treated him really bad if he spilled his milk or cried. My husband started abusing my son when I wouldn't have sex. When he started hurting my son, I started trying to fight back and protect my son, but that only made things worse. He beat both of us worse than ever. He told me that he would call my welfare worker and say that *I* was the one hurting my son if I told the police. He sounded really convincing, and I believed him. He did things like burn my son with hot water in the bathtub while I was tied up on the bed. I lied to the neighbors sometimes, but I think they knew. I was really afraid to let anyone know because I believed that I would lose my son...and now look. I lost him for good. My welfare was cut off because I missed my face–to–face because I was so badly beaten. My son was sleeping a lot and acting like a robot around the house; he was terrified. We didn't have any money, and he [her husband] was beating us every day. I was so sad; I really wanted to call the police, but I didn't think it would help. We'd steal food from the store downstairs, but that was the only time I was outside of the apartment. One day we were all hungry, and my son was crying. He beat him so badly I was really scared. He tied him up and made me have sex while my son was under the bed. When it was over, I rushed to get my son, but he wasn't breathing. He

screamed, "Look what you did, you killed him." That's all I remember. I was crying and screaming for what seemed like a day. The next days were a blur. He moved the baby from room to room, and tried to hide the body in the closet. He was battering me the whole time. I had a breakdown. I didn't eat, sleep, or move for almost a week. When I threatened to tell the truth he went to my grandmother's house and beat her almost to death as a way to keep me quiet. Eventually he took the body outside to bury it, and we went to the police to report my son missing. They didn't believe us for a minute. I was so badly battered that they knew something was up, plus they had the report from my grandmother. At last the police did something.... They arrested us, and I haven't seen my husband since. I was charged with second–degree homicide for failure to protect my child.

As this case illustrates, the women described a pattern of severe physical abuse that escalated over time. All four women I interviewed whose children were killed fit the characteristic gender–entrapment pattern of the African American battered women in the sample.

Their lives had begun with relatively privileged childhood positions in their households of origin. Although two were from economically marginalized families, the four women who shared this path to illegal activities grew up with the sense that as adult women their family life would be a source of pride; it would be within their power to control. As young women, they were confronted with circumstances that created a sense of disenfranchisement and failure in the public sphere, and they began to put more emphasis on their domestic lives.

The onset of abuse from their partners had a disorienting effect on them. Initially, out of loyalty to the men who were abusing them, and later, because of their extreme isolation, only one of the women reached out to her family for help, only one telephoned the police, and each sustained chronic injuries that were exacerbated by lack of treatment and medical mismanagement. In each of the four cases, the violence escalated to a very dangerous level. All of these women were convinced they would ultimately be killed by their batterers. Instead, it was their children who were killed first while the women were virtually held hostage in their homes with no access to the outside world—to a telephone, to a hospital, to their families, or to any social or public services.

Carolyn was a thirty–year–old African American woman, battered by her husband for twelve years. Like Sebina, she was arrested on a homicide charge. She described her situation this way:

> I never did anything illegal, even when I was hungry. My charge is homicide in the first degree, which I am trying to plea down. I'm here because my husband wanted to kill me, and since he couldn't, he killed my baby instead. He knows that I'd rather be dead than have my child dead, so this worked out better for him. I have lost all of my children now, and it will be a slow death for as long as I live knowing that he took the one thing I've ever had as my own. It started one afternoon when I was sleeping in a very deep sleep because he had kept me up for two days in a row. I hadn't been out of his sight for almost three years. Can you imagine that? He locked me in when he went out, and mostly we stayed home. The beatings were a regular part of our life, so when he called me, I was trained to jump up and run to him. This day he told me that our son had fallen and hit his head on the edge of the table. I took one look at him and knew that he hit him with something, and that my son was in serious trouble. He died waiting in the same emergency room that I had been in two nights before after my husband tried to kill me. He wouldn't even let me hold my son as he died. I don't remember what happened after that except that I was screaming that my husband killed my son and that the hospital let him die. My husband was arrested there, and four days later, at my son's funeral, I was arrested and brought to Rikers Island. He told the detectives that *I* hit my son on the head with a hammer that the police found in the trash can in our kitchen. They said both of our fingerprints were on it. Maybe they were, but I did not kill my son! Now he has taken everything from me. I've spent my life running from one hit to another. I've been beaten up since I've been here too....Everyone hates a woman who sleeps while her child is being killed. The only reason I don't hate myself is because I don't even exist anymore after twelve years of being abused.

In only one of these cases did the abuser use drugs and alcohol, and he was not using them at the time of the killing. All of the men were employed at the time of the crime, although marginally, and thus maintained public images of strict, harsh, but hardworking men. Even while they were privately brutalizing their families, they appeared to be close to the ideologically normative family types that the women were so deeply committed to and were symbolically rewarded for having accomplished. One household was deeply involved in a religious organization, and Carolyn's husband assumed a leadership role in several community organizations. Carolyn continued:

> My husband was no drug user or anything. He worked in an auto shop below our apartment and made a small but regular living. He was a member of the social club in the neighborhood, and we went to the local church almost every week if I wasn't looking too bad. He'd even go so far to have his friends over for cards, and I'd be locked in the bedroom, but they didn't think it was unusual. No one really liked him, but he was out in our city doing things that people respected, and that's what fooled them. It also meant that he had more support when it was his word against mine. Since I hadn't talked to anyone in years, they all thought I had gotten weird or snooty. It was easy to blame me. Even my family had given up trying to stay in touch with me since he would never let me see or talk to them. I must have seemed so changed to them—no longer the bubbly, good girl I used to be. Even I didn't know what to believe.

Gender entrapment immobilized these women. In these extraordinarily abusive relationships they committed crimes initially because they misinterpreted their partners' jealous control over them as the type of affection that was consistent with emotional experiences from their younger lives. The women felt as if they gained additional status from their steady relationships and "stable" family lives, especially compared to other members of the household.

As Nicole, a thirty–one–year–old African American women who was arrested on a homicide charge after being battered for four years, said:

> I was the only girl in my family to settle down and get married. From the outside, it looked like things were going as planned. . .June Cleaver, here I come. My folks loved it, especially

having grandchildren. I thought to myself... well, if I have to take a little abuse, it's worth it. My family respected me because I got a "good man"... little did they know! I was getting really scared. The beatings were getting really rough, and he was getting us into illegal stuff, but since I'd lost contact, there was no one to tell. Besides, who'd believe he *made* me rip people off? Not me, no never. He had the phone taken out, and cut my contact with my folks. He went everywhere with me, which they thought was cool—like he was being a good man. I didn't have a single chance to run from him; he watched my every step.

As Nicole's account suggests, the women whose lives took this path to illegal activities felt that the combination of family expectations, fear for their lives, extreme physical trauma, and the constant control of mobility left them too isolated and afraid to reach out for help. However, being implicated in the death of their children was, by far, worse than any direct assault or shame they experienced. They may spend the rest of their lives in prison, living with the legacy of the death of their children for which they felt, in part, responsible. Their stories indicated that this knowledge was the most traumatic form of abuse they endured.

PATH 2. PROJECTION AND ASSOCIATION
"I'll never let a man touch me again."

The life–history interviews revealed a second path that was associated only with the gender entrapment of the African American battered women in this study: being arrested for violent crimes directed at men *other* than the batterer in a symbolic or projected retaliation for past abuse. Four of the women's accounts of their participation in illegal activities centered on the theme, "I'll never let a man touch me again." Their stories illustrated the anger, humiliation, acute physical injury, emotional damage, and long–term legal consequences that resulted from abuse by an intimate partner.

Janet, a forty–six–year–old African American woman, was arrested on a homicide charge. Having been battered by her husband for ten years, she described the following sequence of events:

It took me a long time to get angry, but my anger is actually what got me in big trouble. I decided that no man would ever hit me again like that. Never. So one night when I was visiting my grandmother, my cousin accused me of stealing some money from her. My cousin was drunk, and he was blaming me because *he* took it. I think he was picking on me because I was always the favorite child in the family, and he was jealous. I was so mad that I left the apartment, and he chased me into the street, pushed me, yelled at me, pulled my hair and eventually he started beating me, trying to pick a fight. He hit me in the head, and I lost consciousness. He was still hitting me when I came around, and I just lost my mind, flashing back to when my husband used to sit on my stomach and slap my face. I took a metal stick I always carry in my bag and beat him in the head over and over again. I really didn't mean to kill him; I just lost my mind, and this terror came over me. There were witnesses and everything, but no one came to help until I really started hitting *him*. Did they try to help me? No! They knew that he was my little cousin, so I guess that they thought I didn't need help. I might not have flashed if they had helped me. The judge used the witnesses' lack of help as evidence that I was beating him more than he was beating me… "undue force," they call it. I'm very sorry that I killed him. I know it was my fault, but it was also the fault of my husband. What about his undue force? That's where I learned. They found grandmother's money in my cousin's jacket pocket later that night.

Melanie is a twenty–seven–year–old African American woman who was battered by her husband for six years. She was also detained on a homicide charge. Her story had elements in common with Janet's. She said:

I was arrested for an attempted killing. A man was on my fire escape outside my bedroom window one night, and I shot him. I thought it was my husband returning after three months. He had used weapons to threaten the children, he tried to suffocate me and raped me almost every other day. I have this big scar on my arm from his throwing knives at me. He left after I finally reported him to the police, and that's when the threats started. He'd follow me, stalk my children, call and threaten us on the phone. He broke in my mother's house and drained my bank account. I had to quit my job, because he would show up there and cause trouble with my co-workers. I was broke and late on my rent, and my super was harassing me, wanting me to have sex with him for the back rent. I was getting scared of all men, and when I saw the man on the fire escape, I thought it was one of them trying to get me. As it was, it was the phone man. I don't know what he was doing there after dark, but it doesn't matter. I shot and killed him, and since he was white and I am Black you know what the detectives thought about that! I'm here because I was scared into thinking that any man on the fire escape was trying to get me. It may sound wacky, but it is true that I thought my life was about to end. My husband made me that crazy.

As in the stories of African American women whose partners killed their children, the gender entrapment that began with the gender–identity development as privileged children in their families resulted in these African American women being vulnerable to violent African American men in intimate relationships as adults. Their sense of themselves shifted after the women came to understand that their intimate relationships had, indeed, betrayed them. In the five cases of women who violently assaulted men other than their abusers, their identities shifted again: from a sense of loyalty to men, to humiliation and fear to feelings of anger and frustration. Ironically, in the end, they felt more like their younger, more self–assured, entitled selves.

As Selma's story illustrates, however, this confidence did not work in their favor in the criminal justice system. She was a thirty–year–old African American woman awaiting trial on a weapons and aggravated assault charge after being battered by her husband for six years. She said:

I shot a man who was trying to steal my jacket. But I couldn't prove it, and I didn't act sorry enough when the police arrived. No, he was wrong, not me, and I wasn't going to put on any sorry act in front the cops. I'm through with that act. I'm involved in a grievance here now. It's against an officer who threatened me when I wouldn't take my Keffie off. He said, "Take that rag off your head, darkie." I tricked him into repeating it so that other inmates heard him. Now I'm on the bad list for stepping out of line... but I won't let my dignity be questioned by anyone again, especially someone who is not my family. I am through with compromising myself for some man's sense of power. Even my male lawyer tried to get me to not wear my Keffie to court. He told me that I should not say that I am a Muslim. No, I won't deny myself anymore.... You can't live that way. I won't change for any man ever, ever again. I learned my lesson through the "school of hard knocks," as my mother would say. From perfect child to battered wife to outspoken prisoner.... This has been quite a journey.

From these and the other three accounts that fit this pathway, it can be seen how, when some women were the constant victims of abuse, enduring years of denial, rationalization and failed efforts to change the abuser, they responded almost instinctively to protect themselves from other men. Even though none of the five women fought back in their abusive relationships, and none had committed violent crimes *before* the abuse from their intimate partners, the abuse they experienced was a factor in the women acting aggressively or violently toward men who threatened or attempted to hurt them. This created a particular problem for the gender entrapment of the African American battered women whose paths to Rikers Island were non–domestic assault because: 1) nowhere in the penal code or in the social consciousness is there allowance for this type of crime, 2) the women were likely to encounter potentially violent men on a fairly regular basis given the random violence in communities they lived in and the general rate of street violence and harassment of women, and 3) that racial stereotypes of African American women as aggressive and unfeminine fed into a biased response from the criminal justice authorities.

The stories of women whose experiences fit this pattern revealed how the early message from their families about the importance of taking care of themselves resurfaced and was incorporated into their adult consciousness *after* being battered. The findings indicated that two of these women described attempts to secure help while they were being battered and were directly or indirectly informed that their experiences were relatively unimportant. The women ultimately felt that the best way to resolve their problems was to "take care of their own business," which is why, during the later attempted assaults, they responded in ways that, from the judicial perspective, seemed like extreme uses of violence on *their* part.

Selma continued:

> When I tried to explain to the court about how afraid I was and why I shot the phone man on the fire escape, they seemed to think that I was crazy! My lawyer didn't even bring up the fact that I was battered for six years. He said it didn't have anything to do with what happened. But, for me, it explains why I shot that man. I would have *never* done anything like that if I wasn't well trained by my family to take care of myself and if I hadn't learned from my husband that men will do anything to get me, and I'd better to try to protect myself when a man was coming to hurt me.

PATH 3. SEXUAL EXPLOITATION
"He used sex as a weapon against me."

The third path that characterized a pattern in the population of women interviewed for this study were those women who were arrested and detained for crimes associated with illegal sex work. It is important to note that the life–history interviews revealed that many women in the overall sample were or had been prostitutes or call girls, or had sex for drugs. Some women felt compelled to use their sexuality as a bargaining strategy with police officers, probation officers, or employers because sex was the only source of commerce that they felt they had. Indeed, the sex industry, in all its forms, is a multimillion dollar, international industry, and the women interviewed for this book had a wide range of experiences in it. However, factors such as age, race/ ethnicity, class, and the type of sex work form a distinct hierarchy that dictates which women are vulnerable to arrest for sex work and, once arrested, who is actually charged and detained for these crimes.

Nine battered women interviewed for this study had experiences that led them on this path to illegal activities. There was little distinction by race/ethnicity. Six were African American women charged with prostitution or loitering with intention to prostitute and three were white women. One was charged with sexual harassment, one with prostitution, and one with sexual abuse of a minor. At the time of the interviews, they were facing a range of possible sentences, determined in part by their previous records and the nature of the crime.

Doreen, a twenty–six–year–old African American woman who was arrested for prostitution, was battered by her boyfriend for five years. Her account was typical of the battered women who were arrested for illegal sex work. She described her experience this way:

> In addition to being battered, he used to rape me. Then he'd say that I was such a good slut that I might as well get paid for it, and he'd bring men home and ask them for money to have sex with me. About a year after that started, he took me out to work the street. When I'd get home, the only thing that would stop the abuse was if I brought in lots of money from hooking. Sometimes I would go to work even though I was in pain just so that he would stop beating me for a while. My body hurt all over, but I had to try to make enough money to please him. I was sick a lot, but he'd never let me see a doctor. My life was hell. I was raped by my husband, then forced to prostitute, raped while waiting for a john, had my money stolen by other girls, with frequent infections, cold, drugged out... it was the worst life you can imagine. Since I've been here I found out I have HIV, PID, and lots of other problems. I'm an addict and an alcoholic. I didn't start out this way. My life was going to be very different from this. I was going to go to college to become a teacher. He's stolen my dreams. I've lost my family, my eyesight in one eye, and my outlook on the world as a good place to live. I hope I die soon.

As discussed in the previous chapters, the life–history interviews confirmed that sexuality was indeed a vulnerable aspect of both the African American and the white battered women's lives since many had been sexually abused as young girls and also raped by the men with whom they lived. All but one of the women in this study who were arrested for illegal involvement in the sex industry had a history of sexual abuse as children or as adults by other men in addition to being abused by their husbands or boyfriends. For five of them, the initial violation was by an adult male relative in their families of origin. The other six of the women were raped by strangers, three by more than four different men.

Kim was a thirty–seven–year–old African American woman detained on a prostitution charge. She was battered by her husband for twelve years. She said:

> I was gang–raped by three men in the lobby of my building when I was coming in from work late one night. It was my third time; the first was when I was nine. I think my husband set the whole thing up, because he wasn't the least bit sorry for me. No, he beat me for being raped. From there he started thinking that I should make money having sex with lots of men, so I became a prostitute in our own apartment. It was a good way to make money, but it was almost my death sentence because he used being a prostitute as an excuse for beating me. Working the streets was really safer for me because at least I'd be away from him— across the street trying to get picked up for a while. I didn't care who did what to me; other men using my body became a way to get a break from him. But he used my sex against me in the end. I think he turned me in to the undercover in exchange for them letting him slide in a drug bust.

When the women were sexually abused and then forced into prostitution, pornography, or other sex work, it served as a particularly insidious form of violation, especially when it was criminalized and punished by detention for the battered women and *not* for their pimps (usually the batterer) or their "johns" (the customers)—both groups of which are in a position to profit from forced sex work.

Gwen, a thirty–three–year–old white woman who was battered by her husband for seven years, was detained on a charge of prostitution and sexual abuse of a minor. She described her risks and her husband's benefits this way:

> The hitting of me wasn't the worst part for me; it was filming my daughter dancing naked. At first I didn't get what was going on, because he didn't let me see the films. But then I saw them, and he was making her act like she was dancing in a club, inserting a carrot into her vagina, squeezing her small tits together to make them look bigger, and he made her act like she was masturbating while he filmed her. I don't know for a fact that he was having sex with her. I do know that her gonorrhea must have come from somewhere! He told the cops that I knew what

was going on, that I was a hooker and so they arrested me because I am her guardian. He was just a man making money in the porn business, and I was a prostituting mother who "let" her daughter be filmed. So who goes to jail? I do. I didn't "let" her do anything! He was trying to kill me every day. I was trying to stay alive so that I could *protect* my kids. When I told him I was going to tell, he'd hold a knife to my neck and say that I would be the one to blame... and look, he was right.

The accounts of women whose path to criminal activity was forced sex work illustrate a commonality between the African American and the white battered women. The twelve women who were involved in the criminal justice system because of being pressured into prostitution, forced involvement of their children in pornography, or sexual harassment felt a sense of alienation from their bodies and an internalization of the degradation associated with early and/or repeated sexual victimization. Their treatment within the criminal justice system mirrored the rape and abuse they experienced on the outside. The factor that distinguished the African American battered women from the white women was the *degree* to which the white women had somewhat more control over their working conditions and their income. They tended to be more episodic prostitutes than the African American battered women, who felt forced into illegal sex work on a regular basis—usually nightly.

The gender–entrapment theory that links women's identity development in their households of origin and violence in their intimate relationships to their participation in illegal activities provides a context for understanding how both the African American and the white battered women could be forced into working illegally in the sex industry, how they could become exploited by the men who profit from their illegal activities, and how they might end up detained in a correctional facility for this "criminal" behavior. Sexuality became a source of vulnerability for these battered women, and when that vulnerability was taken advantage of, the women felt very little control over one of the most basic aspects of their selves, their sexual beings.

PATH 4. FIGHTING BACK
"I was not trying to set the apartment on fire."

The fourth path to criminal activities was exemplified by the women whose crimes were arson or other property damage, and assaults of their batterers during an abusive episode. While those women described the incidents as "accidents," they did not deny their involvement with the crimes for which they were charged. The three African American women and two white women whose experiences fit into this category were all battered, and their experiences most closely approximated the experiences of "battered women defendants": battered women who fight back and sometimes kill their batterers in self–defense during or directly following an assault.

April, for example, was a thirty–year–old African American woman who was battered by her husband for six years. Detained on an arson charge, she said:

> We were living on the train waiting for a HPD apartment. He had cooled out a bit, wasn't hitting me so much and I thought things were getting better. When we finally got assigned an apartment, we moved in even though it wasn't finished. We didn't have any electricity, and the construction wasn't complete, so there were holes in the walls and rats running everywhere. It was so upsetting; we were broke, scared, and the tension started building. Of course, he started in on me again. It was bad; I was really getting it. My nose was broken, my body was all bruised, and he was using weapons like he was crazy. One night he was really on me and I yelled to him that I would kill him if he didn't leave me alone. The neighbors upstairs heard me, and that was the evidence they used to arrest me for arson after we knocked a candle over during the fight. I was not trying to set the apartment on fire at all. I was just trying to kick him and kicked it over instead. We both got out and a few hours later the cops picked me up in the park. No one was hurt in the fire, but they said I intentionally set it and then fled.... They must have seen the "Burning Bed" or something. They could tell I'd been hit, given my black eyes and the scars on my face, but it didn't matter in my case. He's on the outside, and I'm facing a trial on an arson charge just for trying to get him off my back.

In the case of all the African American and white women who were arrested for personal or property crimes, the crimes occurred during an assault on them by their batterers. The factors that distinguish the African American battered women's experiences is the isolation that resulted from negative experiences with social services or their families, which led them to believe that they would not be protected by outsiders. And so they felt compelled to protect themselves. The white women did use public services; hence, they had documentation of the abuse. The African American battered women were treated more harshly in the criminal justice system than the white women, who were more likely to be considered victims defending themselves. The African American battered women acted in a more aggressive, self–protective manner, and therefore they were not considered "real" battered women or treated as "victims of crimes." Ironically, the African American battered women were thus trapped by their gender now in the opposite way than in their early life— they were no longer "good girls." Comments from the judges and jurors and advice from their lawyers illustrated this point.

April continued:

> I was told to act like a little white girl... to look sad, to try to cry, to never look the jury in the eye. It didn't really work for me because the judge took one look at me and said, "You look pretty mean; I bet you could really hurt a man."

When compared to the other groups of battered women, the African American and white battered women whose experiences fit this profile were the least severely abused. This group of African American battered women felt that privileges in their households of origin were more material and less emotional and that their commitment to meeting the dominant ideological gender role was less intense, although it was still influential in their sense of themselves. The relevant point for the gender–entrapment theory is that the African American women who were arrested for injury they inflicted during an assault were closest in gender–identity development and abuse profile to the African American women who were not battered, and the white battered women were generally treated more like the "real" battered women than the African American battered women.

PATH 5. POVERTY
"I needed the money and the things."

The fifth pathway of the women's involvement in illegal activities was characterized by those women who were arrested for property crimes and other economically motivated crimes. All of the women in this study who were detained on charges of burglary, robbery, possession of stolen property, and forgery were African American. Five were battered and forced into illegal activities, and one was not battered. The five battered women whose experiences fit this profile had startlingly similar stories.

Consider Inca, a thirty–one–year–old African American woman who was detained on a burglary charge. She was battered by her husband for seven years. Inca said:

> The abuse got so bad that it was getting hard for me to keep going to work. Since we needed the money, this only made him more upset, and I was getting really desperate. I started working for a white family who had more than enough things, so I started lifting food and clothes. They would just leave money around, and once he came there to finish an attack he started the night before and he saw the money and took it and some jewelry. He said he had no respect for me being a maid and all, and that he'd think more of me if I put my "slave work" to use for us. So I began to move from job to job every few months to steal stuff. He'd sell it and keep the money. He was beating me and harassing me and teasing me all the while, unless I made a good boost. It was like we were working together for the first time. The only time I felt really good was when he was spotting for me. It was like he was acting like a real husband for the first time, and I got sucked into feeling protected and taken care of. Since I was the one stealing, I've served time twice before for possession of stolen property and burglary. But he was the one who set it up. He was the one who beat me if I didn't get the goods, and he never even visits me when I'm here. My pride is hurt more than my body. All of my dreams have been ruined forever, and I don't think very much of myself anymore. I went from a winner to a thief really fast.

The life–history interviews with African American battered women arrested for economically motivated crimes revealed that one of the ways that the men coerced the women into crime was to portray *themselves* as more vulnerable to law enforcement and to portray the women as better situated to commit crimes. This key aspect of gender entrapment fits into the frame of reference established in the women's households of origin. The African American men used the fact of their overrepresentation in the criminal justice system and other racial rhetoric to strike a chord of sympathy with the African American battered women. So in those families where *someone* "needed" to steal, the women felt that it should be them instead of their male partners. Most of the women recalled that they knew, on some level, that they were being manipulated by cultural ideology, but their clarity and judgment were impaired by the truth in the statistical picture on which their batterers were depending as well as by their own family loyalties, the emotional consequences of abuse, and the fear of physical assault. This paradoxical set of circumstances is at the core of the gender–entrapment theoretical model.

Jeanne, a thirty–five–year–old African American women detained on a burglary charge, was battered by her boyfriend for seven years. She described her situation in these words:

> The first time I got arrested I actually felt proud. The cops caught us running out of the store with the goods in my bag. I was six months' pregnant because he had raped me, and I knew that if they took him, he would surely get time, and the baby wouldn't have a father.... So much for the perfect family I wanted. Also I believed what he told me, "They'd never keep a pregnant woman in jail." Well, that was one of the many lies he told me. Yes, they've kept me here, and, no, they haven't treated me any better than anyone else. I slept on the floor of the bull pen the first night, I never get any milk, and the clothes they gave me don't fit. And speaking of the courts, they don't treat Black women any better than Black men! I guess I knew what the deal was, but since I couldn't understand why I was allowing myself to be battered, at least his lines made it easier to take the abuse. It was as if I talked myself into believing that the hitting, the punching, the put–downs, and even the crime made sense since he was a Black man. Like I somehow owed this to him because of how my life had been easier than his. Was it really? Well, yes and no. *Now* it isn't, that's for sure.

For some of the women charged with economically motivated crimes, the illegal activities were the family's only source of income. Poverty and lack of employment motivated their activities. For others, the economically motivated illegal activities provided an ironic sense of justice for discriminatory employment practices or humiliating occupational experiences. For others still, the crimes represented an opportunity for mutuality and shared power with their abusers, different from their legal, public life where *she* felt privileged, or their domestic life, where *he* was abusive.

Beverly, a thirty–three–year–old African American woman who was detained on a burglary charge, was battered by her common–law husband for twelve years. She said:

> I was working in an all–white neighborhood cleaning house. I felt humiliated by people when I went shopping or when I would stand near them on the train...like I somehow looked like I was about to steal something. That's how Black men feel all the time I think. The white people I worked for may have trusted me, but their friends and neighbors dissed (disrespected) me all the time. It reinforced the way that my husband talked about my work. He really hated white people, and he said they hated me, which was actually true. After he started abusing me and we both lost our jobs, we started playing con games. Our only targets were white people. The only houses we broke into were rich houses, and the only credit cards we lifted were gold cards. It was like we were on a mission. And when the cops found him beating me on the street, wouldn't you know it, they were two white guys, and so he convinced me not to press charges against him for assault.

As the gender–entrapment theoretical model suggests, the African American battered women whose experiences fit this profile rationalized the shame they occasionally felt for their actions by focusing on their feelings of being victimized by racism and poverty. Drawing on their sense of being betrayed by their limited social options, they felt entitled to the resources and property of those with more privilege. Again the theme of African American men's particular vulnerability surfaced to influence the African American women's rationalizations and tolerance of their involuntary involvements in illegal activities. In the end, however, no matter how much money was derived from these illegal activities, in each of these instances, the woman arrived at Rikers Island poor and disheartened. At the time of the interviews, the women were able to reflect on how they were used by the batterers and how their criminal "partnerships" were, indeed, extensions of the abusive and exploitative relationships.

The one African American non–battered woman who was detained on this path had a different experience and analysis of her involvement in illegal activities. She described stealing food, clothing to sell, and tips from restaurant tables as sources of income. In contrast to those whose experiences fit the gender–entrapment model, this woman did not describe her identity or activity as being influenced by loyalty, culturally constructed gender roles, or fear of abuse. Instead, she reported that for her, stealing was a way to make a living that was more profitable than being part of a marginalized labor pool, which she felt was her only other option.

PATH 6. ADDICTION
"I use drugs to numb the pain."

Demographic data profiling women detained at Rikers Island suggest that drug use and a more aggressive criminal justice policy on drug offenses are the primary cause of the drastic increase in the incarceration rates of women. Nine women in this sample were detained on drug–related offenses. Unlike the other five paths, drug offenses were the only ones on which members of all three subgroups were arrested. However, the patterns of drug use and the meaning of illegal drug activities were significantly different for the African American battered women, the white battered women, and the African American non–battered women who were interviewed. A summary of the differences provides an important example of one of the fundamental aspects of the gender–entrapment theoretical model of women's illegal activities—how the women's behaviors were organized by internal factors as well as social circumstances.

Of the four African American battered women arrested on drug offenses, all of them described the battering as preceding their drug use. The women described their use of drugs as a way to establish a deeper connection with their partners, to create emotional intimacy and mutual sexual pleasure with their abusers. While they describe using drugs "of their own free will," they felt that the batterers' addiction and their desire to connect with them was a motivating force into drug use. The women's desperate desire for intimacy and connection, even through illegal activities, was a central theme in their gender entrapment.

Johnetta, a thirty–six–year–old African American woman who was arrested on a drug charge, was battered by her husband for three years. Her story illustrated this point:

> I remember when I shifted from being angry at him or manipulated by him to feeling really scared of him, but my life was already bottoming out too fast for me to do anything. I started trying to calm myself down and trying to get next to him, which I thought would help him not kill me. I was really mixed up. First I thought drugging would make us close, like a real couple. But then I felt scared too. I basically didn't know what the hell I was doing except trying, trying, trying to make things all right for me and my man. I hated the taste of alcohol and how it made me feel, so I started with heroin. At first, it worked. I wasn't so scared; he was very hot for sex with me, and then he'd sleep a lot. Even if he did beat me, it didn't seem to hurt as much when I was high, so I thought of it as "medicating" and caring for myself. I started using dope every day, and soon it was eating up all of our money. When we didn't have money for the drugs, I was in real trouble because his abuse got really out of control. So I started selling as a way to keep us supplied. We kept needing more drugs, and he stopped being able to perform sex, and so that wasn't working like it used to calm him down. The violence continued to get worse, and I was really getting scared, but police and family help were less helpful than ever. So I'm here, safe from him at least, but addicted to heroin and trying to detox. He's probably beating up another woman, getting her addicted now too.

Like Johnetta, several other women in this category felt as if the violence initially decreased when they were using drugs with their partners, which served as an incentive to continue using drugs in order to avoid being battered.

The other two African American women who were arrested on drug charges attributed the onset of their drug use more directly to being physically battered. One was injected with an intravenous drug by her batterer as he physically restrained her. The other was forced to use drugs as her batterer threatened her with a knife; she became addicted to street morphine when the batterer began to give it to her for pain relief.

Blondie, a twenty–one–year–old African American woman detained on a drug charge, was battered by her boyfriend for four years. Her experience of being battered, forced to use drugs, and then arrested fit the classic pattern of gender entrapment. She said:

> I would be in serious pain and couldn't stop screaming. At first I denied and tried to hide the abuse, but he would beat me to keep me quiet! But sometimes I'd have broken bones, so I couldn't just be quiet. He would go out and come home with "medicine," which I think was initially legit, and I fell for his acting like he was taking care of me. He'd shoot me up with it. He started buying morphine on the street. It really helped the physical pain and the emotional pain. And soon I needed more and more to numb the pain of broken bones that weren't set, including a broken arm. Now I try to get it on my own even when he isn't beating me because I am addicted. I wanted him to care so badly! I was used to being cared for. So at first the fact that he cared enough to get the drugs was more important than that he beat me, especially because he told me all along about how he beat me because he cared. I don't really get it, but now I'm an addict because he cared so much? I don't think so!

The four African American non–battered women who were arrested on drug charges presented a different profile. Most were introduced to illegal drugs by a peer group instead of an individual, and described their initiation to drug use as voluntary rather than coerced. But their stories were similar to the African American battered women who experienced the rapid decline into addiction that characterizes the use of crack cocaine and heroin (the drugs of choice of most of the women I interviewed who used drugs), especially when these drugs were combined with morphine, alcohol, and methadone to create a debilitating and expensive habit. Unlike the African American battered women, however, this subgroup became involved in selling drugs for their own profit and tended to use drugs as a public and social rather than private activity, distinguishing the meaning of drug use for those women whose experiences fit the model of gender entrapment and those whose illegal drug use did not.

Anita, a thirty–five–year–old African American woman who was not battered and was detained on a felonious drug charge, illustrated the meaning of drug use when violence was not present. She said:

> Getting high for me was a way to pass the time having fun with the people who mattered most to me. We'd buy some dope, maybe buy a bottle and go to someone's house to spend the day. We were always careful to include those who were really strung out because they needed the fix more than we did, at first. I knew I was using too much and that I was probably not going to be able to stop very easily, but it was the best... maybe the only way to be connected to this group of people. And they were like family until things got really bad and I one of the strung–out ones who was invited along out of pity. It got real bad, but it could have been worse. Dope took over my life—no, I gave my life over to the dope. I wouldn't do it again, but hey, we all make mistakes. I never hurt anyone except myself. And no one ever hurt me but myself. I'm trying to get my life together now. I think I'll make it this time.

The one white battered woman who was detained on a drug–related charge was the only woman in this sample who was not addicted to the drugs she sold. Her story illustrates the complicated relationship between poverty and the economics of the illegal drug trade, even when addiction was not part of the experience. Linda was a thirty–three–year–old white woman who was battered by her husband for nine years. While detained for possession of an illegal substance, she said:

> There is one and only one reason I am here.... I sold drugs to try to get an apartment. The undercovers who busted me knew that I was not an addict, but I guess they didn't care. They need a certain number of arrests before they can go home. I had lots of drugs on me, and I was about to cop lots of money.... That's all they needed to know. I tried working, but my husband found out, beat me up, and took my money. There were lots of drugs in our neighborhood, and so it wasn't hard to find customers and suppliers. I never had an identity as a dealer, but I was starting

to save enough to move out. No one, so far, has believed me that I only did it as a way to get away from him. Oh well, at least being here I'm away.

The issues of addiction and battering are complicated ones for both the women and the social agencies designed to help them. The political economy of the illegal drug trade in this country complicates matters further. For the purposes of this study, it is important to note that drug use, poverty, criminal justice policy, and incarceration create a deeply tangled web into which many battered women in this study fell. This set of circumstances accelerated gender entrapment for some of the African American battered women and, like several of the other paths to illegal activities, will have lasting consequences for their lives.

A SUMMARY OF GENDER ENTRAPMENT AND ILLEGAL ACTIVITY

The women's stories revealed that their paths to illegal activities were determined by multiple factors, including their early childhood experiences, the construction of a cultural/racial identity, critical events in the public sphere, the presence or absence of violence in their intimate relationships, and responses from social institutions. These factors, described as antecedent events in this chapter, varied by race/ethnicity and experience of abuse, thereby distinguishing the three subgroups and their vulnerabilities to gender entrapment.

Four circumstances that the African American battered women experienced provided the empirical illustration of the gender–entrapment theoretical model of women's illegal activities. Their criminal activities, first and foremost, were seen by them as responses to violence or the threat of violence in their intimate relationships. Letisha, a thirty–seven–year–old African American battered woman detained on a forgery charge, said:

I know it's hard for people to believe, but I really thought he would kill me if I refused to go along with his scheme. I really, really did. He had tried before, and I think he wanted to ruin my life so badly he'd resort to either death or by sending me upstate for life. I got tricked into all of this by being naive, nice and because I tried to take care of him. But you'd really have to know how brutal he was, how afraid I was of him, and how little anyone seemed to be able to do to help. The risk of being arrested was much less scary for me than being killed by my husband. I know it's hard to believe, but it's better for me here than on the outside where I have to face him and my failed life.

Most of the African American battered women described the illegal activities as ways to postpone a violent episode, although they did not see them as ways to avoid being battered altogether. The African American battered women did what they were told whether it was legal or not, because they believed that not to do so would cause them more severe physical harm or emotional distress or, in some instances, even death. In this sense, they continued to be the good girls they had learned to be in childhood.

A second element of gender entrapment is illustrated by the ways that the African American battered women committed crimes as extensions of their internalized gender roles and their strong sense of racial identity. The African American battered women's experiences were so complicated by feelings of loyalty to the men who were battering them that even as they were being abused and coerced into crime, they were working hard to create intimacy in their relationships and stability in their domestic lives. Illegal activities, for some of them, enhanced their sense of closeness, of mutuality, of being involved in shared work. Ironically, their criminal activities demonstrated their allegiance to the violent men with whom they were intimately involved. In return, they kept expecting that their relationships would be enhanced and that the violence would ultimately end. Indeed, some were occasionally rewarded with the kind of attention and gratitude they were used to. Their sense of failure, stigma, and shame ironically kept them *in* the criminal life rather than out of it.

Shelia, a twenty–eight–year–old African American battered woman detained on a burglary charge, said:

Funny, but when we were in the life was the best time of our life. It was when we were the closest, when I trusted him most, and when he needed me. I was hurt a lot by the way he treated me, especially that he took me away from my family and the dream of the family we could have had together. But when we were working together, I thought there was at least a chance.

And I thought if we could just get ourselves on our feet, everything would be all right with us. It was a way to work on the
dream—to be in crime with him. You'd be surprised what you'd
do when love and fear are put together into one home.

A third motivation for illegal activities that is a characteristic
of the gender–entrapment model is that some women abided by
the culturally constructed perception that African American
women's role was to be protective of African American men
who, indeed, were vulnerable to the effects of institutionalized
racism. Interspersed with descriptions of their pain and shame,
some women proudly expressed rhetoric about the "protection of
the Black family through the protection of the Black man."
While sophisticated in their political and economic analysis of
racism, these women were the least insightful about their positions as *women* in the context of a racially and gender–stratified
social order.

Lila was a fifty–four–year–old African American battered
woman detained on a burglary charge. She said:

Through him I was becoming aware of my Blackness. I decided
that part of being a "race woman" was having a relationship
with a man who was strongly identified with Black politics and
who had paid the consequences of racism. So, as an ex–con, he
was perfect. Prison taught him to be angry, and my role was to
soften him up again by taking on the stronger role. My goal was
to make him a king, and I became his sugar mama. He was using drugs that he was introduced to while serving time. He was
very violent, which he said he also learned in the slammer. But I
began to work to take care of him, but it wasn't enough. He
forced me into prostitution, which was the only thing he knew
about women's work. The abuse got worse and worse, and I was
feeling like a failure, so I left town as a way to get away. He followed me to Florida and, away from my family and friends, I was
even more badly treated by him. But I kept trying to make him
better. We read *Malcolm X* together, went to meetings and tried
to bond about political things. My first arrest was there by a
judge for being battered.... He said he was tired of his cops coming to my house, and so, since I refused to press charges, he arrested me. Can you believe it? It was the first sign that being a
sugar mama would not work.... The deck was stacked against

me as a Black woman, and being a kingmaker just wasn't possible no matter how I tried.

Lastly, some of the African American battered women, particularly those with a previous record, intentionally got arrested or turned themselves in as a strategy to avoid the abuse. Six African American battered women described this factor as directly leading to their arrests, while other women expressed a sense of relief that in jail they were safe for the first time in many years from the violence in their intimate relationships. This indicated two troubling ironic trends, of women and men using the criminal justice system to meet basic survival needs, such as food and shelter, and how functional the involvement with illegal activities have become. For the population of women in this study whose experiences were consistent with gender entrapment, jail became one of the few sources of safety from abusive male partners that they could envision.

Crystal, a twenty–seven–year–old African American battered women detained on an arson charge, said:

> I would have never thought it was true, but it's much better for me here than on the outside. In addition to "three hots and a cot," I have protection from him. He tried to get to me, but since he can't call, and I can refuse visits, and they search visitors, I am as safe from him here as I have ever been. I'm not saying it's a good place to be, but for women like me, it's better than living without guards.

The African American non–battered women in this study whose experiences did not fit the gender–entrapment model committed crimes as an extension of peer relationships and addiction. Their accounts of their involvements in illegal activities suggested that they were also influenced by their identity formation in their households of origin, the construction of their racial/ethnic identities, and their perceptions of their social location in the public sphere. However, having grown up in marginalized families, they felt the limitations of poverty, racism, and lack of social opportunity at a young age, and they internalized identities that were consistent with this world view. The one way that this worked in their favor, ironically, was that the African American women who were not battered did not compromise their own safety, health, happiness, or indeed legal status for intimate relationships. As such, they were less vulnerable to abuse and not forced by violence or the threat of violence into the illegal activities for which they had been arrested.

Each of the white battered women I interviewed for this book also participated in one of the six paths to illegal activities in response to the threat of violence in their intimate relationships. What distinguished their experiences from the gender–entrapment model that characterized the African American battered women's experiences was that the white women were involved in crime as a way *out* of the violent relationships, whereas the African American battered women were trapped in criminal activity in much the same way that they were trapped in their intimate relationships. While some of the white battered women were motivated by their early childhood experiences, their identities, and their fear of trying to separate from their batterers' illegal activities, the African American battered women were drawn to participate in crime as a way to end the violence but not necessarily the relationships.

By contrasting the backgrounds and experiences of the three subgroups in this sample in terms of the gender–identity development, violence in their intimate relationships, and, in this chapter, the paths they took to illegal activities, the key elements of the gender–entrapment process were illustrated. In the next chapter, the theoretical model that I call gender entrapment is reviewed and summarized as an alternative explanation of some African American battered women's participation in illegal activities.

6

THE STORY OF
GENDER ENTRAPMENT

Considering the Context

IN THIS chapter I tell the composite story of gender entrapment: the common factors and general patterns that the interviews with the three subgroups of women at Rikers Island Correctional Facility revealed. I do so to help readers understand that while each woman's story is important and insightful, none represents an "isolated case" or "odd aberration." Indeed, when taken together, the women's stories clearly portray a series of circumstances that had many shared dimensions, and many of the women assigned like meanings to comparable events.

In this chapter, I use *my* words to describe the pattern, comparable events and dimensions that are shared. In it, I focus on how the dialectic of the dominant ideology about intimate heterosexual relationships in contemporary society and the social conditions in African American communities converge to create a *particular* dilemma for African American battered women. When considered against the backdrop of the three trends discussed in Chapter One, the choices they faced and decisions that had to be made among very poor options gets clearly revealed as a setup—the gender entrapment of the African American battered women which compelled them to crime.

The gender–entrapment paradigm is illustrated most vividly when the experiences of the African American women who are battered are distinguished from members of the other two populations of incarcerated women I interviewed. The chapter is organized to highlight these differences. It begins, however, with a review of the gender–entrapment theoretical model.

THE GENDER-ENTRAPMENT THEORETICAL MODEL

As previously stated, the theory of gender entrapment developed here appropriates its meaning from the legal notion of entrapment, which implies a circumstance whereby an individual is lured into a compromising act. When applied to battered women who commit crimes, I use the term gender entrapment to describe what happens to women who are marginalized in the public sphere because of their race/ethnicity, gender, and class and are then battered by their male partners. The model helps to show how some women are forced or coerced into crime by their culturally expected gender roles, the violence in their intimate relationships, and their social position in the broader society. The model, which was based on the life–history interviews of African American battered women as compared and contrasted with African American non–battered women and white women, is built upon elements of: 1) the feminist theories of identity development;[1] 2) culturally relative and African American feminist approaches to the study of the family in contemporary society;[2] and 3) social constructionist explanations of gender–role behavior as emotional work.[3] By adding violence and crime as variables, the theory enables a more precise explanation of the experiences of African American battered women—a subset of the overall population of incarcerated women and one that has been seriously neglected by the dominant social–science research and the feminist based anti–violence movement.[4]

As described in the previous chapters, during the life–history interviews I focused on the ways that the women tried to assert their own desires and needs, as well as how their early childhood experiences, emotional processes and the perceptions they had of their social options influenced and regulated their behaviors. The concept of gender entrapment is based on all of these forces, as well as the dynamics among them. The epistemological value of the gender–entrapment theoretical model is that it gives equal emphasis to a multiplicity of factors (theoretical approaches *and* social variables) that lead to women's illegal behavior—therefore offering a more textured analysis of the relations between gender–identity development, violence against women, race/ethnicity, and women's involvement in crime.

As the stories indicated, there was a sequential and reciprocal relationship among the properties of the women's households of origin, the cultural contexts of their lives, their adult intimate relationships, and their gender. These relationships made some African American women particularly vulnerable to gender entrapment and protected the other two groups from it.

THE SOCIOLOGICAL CONTEXT OF GENDER–IDENTITY DEVELOPMENT IN THE HOUSEHOLD OF ORIGIN

The structure and function of the women's households, their cultural frame of reference, and the ways that their families were influenced by the dominant social order set the stage for the gender entrapment the African American battered women experienced. In analyzing their gender–identity development in their households of origin, the following five factors emerged from the data to form a distinct and overall pattern of gender entrapment for the African American battered women.

1. Non–hegemonic Gender Roles

With few exceptions, the African American women in this study grew up in households that were *not* organized around hegemonic gender roles. Their stories revealed that this was true for a variety of reasons, including economic necessity, the trauma of family violence, cultural residency patterns, and deliberate decisions to compose households that were more consistent with the culturally relative view of family life.[5]

Most of the battered and non–battered African American women's families of origin did not conform in structure or function to the ideological norm. Some were from households that were comprised only of women. In other families, the older siblings or an adult man served as the primary caretaker of the children. In most of the African American women's households the women worked for wages outside their homes, and reproduction was not necessarily limited to legally sanctioned unions.

The factor that distinguished the African American women who were battered from those African American women who were not battered was the degree to which they *aspired* to the ideological norm. The distinguishing factor between the white battered women and the African American battered women was that the former grew up in a more normative family structure than the latter. The white women's families were typically more patriarchal in form and function; their mothers were seldom part of the paid labor force even though the families were very poor, and the women and girl children assumed traditional gender roles in their households.

2. Aspirations to the Ideological Norm

Despite this apparent divergence from the heterosexual nuclear family form of their families of origin, many of the African American battered women *aspired* to the ideological norm, believing that a "normal" family structure and "normal" gender arrangements would symbolically and materially improve their social status. Those women who grew up in comfortable or privileged positions in their households thought that a traditional nuclear family would mean that their good lives would be even better. For the women whose lives were characterized by extreme poverty or sexual abuse, ideologically normal families were considered a potential way out of their despair. In either case, their yearning and efforts to attain structurally traditional families were important initial elements of gender entrapment.

A deeper analysis of this apparent contradiction reveals the complex effect of ideology on the aspirations of the African American battered women in this study. Most of the women did not express the desire to have family lives that were different from their own because of shame, lack of appreciation for their families, or embarrassment. Ironically, most of the African American battered women felt that the composition of their childhood households would allow them to meet the ideological norm as adults. It was as if the family structure and functioning of their families of origin—their mothers' working outside of the home, their extended families' contribution to the economic base of the household, and their older siblings' assumption of caretaker roles—afforded them the emotional and material opportunity to imagine something different for their futures. A few of those who had a more difficult existence in their households of origin considered the establishment of a traditional family structure as a way to escape their troubled homes. However, they too did not blame their family members for their problematic childhood experiences, focusing instead on the social circumstances that led to poverty, alcoholism, or other problems in their families.

In contrast, the African American women who were not battered did not aspire to or assume that an ideologically normative household would enhance the quality of their lives. Their expectations for adult intimate relationships were more consistent with their experiences as young children, and they did not desire or place as much emphasis on creating a household structurally different from the ones in which they grew up. In particular, the African American non–battered women did not invest energy into establishing long–term, monogamous domestic relationships with men, preferring more episodic romantic and/or peer-like social relationships.

The white women expected to replicate the structure of their households of origin. Like the African American battered women, they expected to participate in traditional gender and generational relationships. What distinguished them from the other two groups was that even though their households of origin were more consistent with dominant ideology, they grew up feeling ashamed of and uncomfortable in their household environments. Unlike the other two groups, the white women tended to attribute their problems to their family background. In the life-history interviews they described ways that the organization of their households of origin was the root cause of the negative conditions in their adult lives, yet they could not conceive of a viable alternative.

3. Lowered Social Status and Lowered Expectations

For most of the African American battered women, neither growing up with emotional support and relative material privilege nor their optimism could mitigate the negative effects of the social world, which is organized hierarchically by race/ethnicity and gender. Reality took its toll early on the African American battered women's lives as their sense of themselves and of the options available to them were limited by institutional forces. Those who did well in school as young children felt the encouragement for academic achievement end before they reached adolescence. Their employment opportunities were limited to "traditional Black women's work," those occupational choices that were consistent with the historically narrow options.[6] Even those women who had less traditional jobs were discouraged by demeaning interactions in their occupational settings because of their gender and race/ethnicity. Some of the African American battered women felt the sting of overt racial and sexual harassment early in their work lives.

The African American women who were not battered also faced discrimination in the social sphere. It had a different effect on them, however, because their lower social status did not come as a surprise to them. They did not grow up feeling special, and their treatment in the public sphere was consistent with their experiences and expectations. The African American non-battered women were more likely to interpret discouraging events and circumstances as evidence of their hopelessly marginalized positions, and they reacted in ways that symbolized "giving up" or "dropping out." In contrast to the African American battered women who began to work harder in the area where they thought they had more control—the private sphere—the non-battered women's pattern was to avoid the types of long–term intimate relationships that the battered women sought in order to compensate for their limited social success and mobility. To understand this central aspect of gender entrapment, it is important to distinguish the African American battered women's high expectations of their *relationships* from their low expectations from *the men* with whom they were involved. Both groups of African American women came to feel generally powerless or vulnerable in the world; however, the African American battered women felt as if they could make their intimate relationships work even without the ability, cooperation, or commitment from the African American men with whom they were involved.

On this item, the pattern for the white battered women was similar to that of African American non–battered women. While they did not experience racial discrimination, their gender and class position left them feeling alienated and outside the mainstream of social life although they felt this was a normal experience for women. They generally had a more isolated existence and did not have much exposure to or expectations of social privileges—the public sphere was the purview of men. Ironically, as in the case of the African American non–battered women, the white women's lower expectations of themselves, their lives, and their relationships protected them from gender entrapment—but not from abuse.

4. Social Basis of Hegemonic Aspiration

The degree to which the women's aspirations for a family were socially constructed has important implications for understanding the gender entrapment of the African American battered women whose stories are told in this book. Their aspirations about family life reflected a broader commitment to traditional Western values and dominant social sentiments than those of the non–battered African American women, and their belief that they could realistically achieve this standard distinguished them from the white battered women. Despite the contemporary conditions in their communities—increasing levels of poverty, the continued discrimination against women and people of color, health problems that have reached epidemic proportions, and a narrowing of the social policies aimed at creating equal opportunity for groups that have been historically discriminated against—many of the African American battered women in the study grew up in a generation where African American people desired and indeed felt the possibility of middle–class status.[7] Their aspirations and the images of themselves as potentially having equal access to society's opportunities, resources, and rewards represented real gains that have benefited groups historically discriminated against in this country.

At the same time, their aspirations also represented the social pressure exerted through mainstream media, educational institutions, public policy makers, and indeed the African American community of middle–class professionals toward one standard of social success. The literature on gender attitudes, for example, suggests that in contrast to the popular notion that has arisen from the feminist movement of the 1970s, young women, including African American women, characteristically associate material comfort, professional attainment, and successful family life with a nuclear, patriarchal family form.[8] For the African American battered women in this study, a woman on her own was almost by definition a poor woman, an unsuccessful woman, and a bad mother. Indeed, this conventional opinion was reinforced by the reality of the social experiences with which the women were familiar and current social–policy proposals aimed at welfare reform. The incorporation of the dominant ideological view into the African American battered women's frames of reference and, ultimately into their sense of themselves and their futures was accomplished at a very young age. The African American women who were later battered were more taken in by these aspirations because they felt privileged and special in their families, unlike the African American women who were not battered and the white battered women who were less hopeful about attaining the benefits commonly associated with middle–class status.

5. *Cultural Reinforcement of Aspirations*

The African American battered women's aspirations were shaped by cultural solidarity and racial awareness as well as dominant ideology. For them, the establishment and maintenance of a nuclear family was seen as not only desirable, but as a way to provide the protective support that they perceived African American families would need against problems in the future. Some African American battered women's views had a distinctly conservative tone, similar to the rhetoric of scholars, public–policy experts, and legislators who criticize alternative family structures in African American communities.[9] Another cluster of responses were from those African American battered women who articulated a neonationalist position, emphasizing one (distinctly patriarchal) interpretation of the principles of recent disciples of Marcus Garvey and Malcolm X.[10]

With striking uniformity, the African American battered women interviewed for this study expressed a loyalty to their families that included solidarity with and, by extension, protection of men to whom racial and economic discrimination was directed. There was a distinct absence of expressed awareness of the women's *own* vulnerabilities to similar social and economic forces as African American *women* in contemporary society. This early solidarity with African American men was contradicted later when the African American battered women described their ambivalence toward men who abused their male privileges and used the perception that they were the most oppressed sector of the community to rationalize their violence.

In contrast, neither the African American non–battered women nor the white battered women were influenced by philosophical or political assumptions that led to feelings of solidarity with men. While the African American non–battered women expressed loyalty to their families and communities, their expressions did not include a sense of being responsible for creating conditions of change. The sentiments expressed by the white battered women diverged even further from African American battered women's. They were alienated from their families, estranged from men in general, and relatively powerless and detached from broader political or social issues. The non–battered African American and the white battered women's vulnerability to gender entrapment was lessened by their perception of themselves and their needs as distinct from the men in their lives, whereas the African American battered women felt more connected to and sympathetic toward men.

THE CONTEXT AND MEANING OF VIOLENCE IN INTIMATE RELATIONSHIPS

Violence against women—particularly within the context of intimate relationships—drastically shifts the structure and meaning of the household unit and radically alters the dynamic of adults' intimate interaction. It affects women's behavior in profound and lasting ways.[11] As such, the onset of violence and its ongoing effects are key factors in the gender–entrapment theoretical model. For the African American battered women in this study, as for most women who experience physical and emotional abuse in the domestic sphere, the onset of violence set in motion a series of complex responses that included internal processes (such as denial) and concrete actions (such as calling the police). These simultaneous and sometimes contradictory responses were not always in the direction of rationality because, as the analysis showed, the internal processes were influenced by their gender–identity development, and the concrete actions were regulated by ongoing institutional practices such as ineffective police responses. Studies on the use of hospital emergency rooms by battered women reveal, for example, that women eventually stop using public services even though their injuries get worse over time.[12] The literature attributed this pattern to the finding that some battered women actually feel worse when the services ignore the violence, as this experience *reinforces* their sense of shame, guilt, and powerlessness.[13]

The analysis of the findings about the physical, emotional, and social consequences of being battered and the subsequent meanings the African American battered women attached to violence in their intimate relationships can be summarized according to six factors that distinguish their experiences as gender entrapment from the other groups in this sample.

1. Pressure to Conform to Ideology

The commitment to dominant ideology and indeed the emotional work and social pressure to conform to it deeply influenced the African American battered women's adult intimate relationships. They, like the white women, were highly influenced by the hegemonic assumptions about the appropriate public and private roles for women, and their attempts to approximate these roles were rewarded intermittently by traditional relationships with men, praise from their families, admiration of their peers, and social status as a "real family."

Most of the African American battered women and the white battered women became involved with one of the first men who expressed or demonstrated an interest in having an intimate relationship with them; however, the African American women felt considerably more pressure to get involved because of their male partners' limited public success. Once in the relationship, both the African American and the white women assumed traditional roles in relation to their male partners: the woman was the nurturer concerned with creating intimacy and providing emotional comfort, while their male partners made most major decisions, initiated sexual activity, and led more active public lives. Accomplishing the tasks traditionally associated with being women in contemporary society consumed a significant amount of their emotional and social resources.

This was particularly true for the African American women, who, like their male counterparts, were more likely to be structurally excluded from most opportunities to express conventional gender roles than the white women and men.[14] The African American battered women's participation in the work force as the primary income producers for their households, for example, was inconsistent with the dominant ideology of women's roles. Even though the African American battered women did work outside their homes, the gendered division of labor in the reproductive sphere was not affected. This included those who did the "work" of securing and maintaining public benefits and those who worked illegally. In each case the African American battered women whose stories are told in this book assumed the burden of household tasks, usually without adequate material resources, and also a significant share of the economic burden.

The literature supports the notion that working outside the home does not necessarily lead to more privileged positions in the private sphere for white women.[15] In the case of African American women, working outside the home may increase their economic independence, but it does not decrease their emotional dependence or desire for interdependence with the men in their lives.[16] Quite the contrary, the African American battered women in this study indicated that the harder they worked outside their homes, the more strongly they held to their fantasies of traditional gender roles and domestic arrangements, which included emphasizing African American men's power, strength, and dominant roles in their families. This commitment later turned into a significant element of risk for gender entrapment.

The white battered women did not need to work as hard to conform to the dominant ideology because their family structures were already consistent with it. In contrast to the African American battered women, who felt compelled to create an *illusion* of a traditional relationship, traditional relationships were the *reality* for white battered women. Ironically, their risk was reduced by their subordinate status to the men in their lives because they expected men to occasionally abuse their power and they were less surprised when they became violent. The white women understood their vulnerability very well.

2. Disbelief and Disorganization

As is characteristic of most battered women, when the violence in their intimate relationships began, the women's initial reaction was disbelief.[17] The onset of physical and emotional abuse so deeply contradicted both the dominant ideology *and* the African American battered women's expectations of their intimate relationships that most of them initially denied the seriousness and rationalized the abuse in hopes that it would eventually stop.[18]   Again, it is important to understand that some of the African American women who were battered as adults grew up with feelings approaching omnipotence, and when their power was threatened by school failure or being underemployed, they directed their hopes for achievement and success to their family lives. Violence simply did not fit with their expectations and hopes for themselves in relationships. Even those women who were abused as children or who saw their mothers abused responded to the early assaults as an aberration rather than an emerging pattern of events in their intimate relationships.

As the violence in their intimate relationships escalated over time, it posed a more serious threat to their sense of self and their accomplishments in the domestic sphere. Most of the African American battered women described the precise moment when their identities changed from "successful female intimate partners working on their dreams" to "victims of a circumstance over which they could not gain control." It is significant to note that most of the African American battered women did not consider themselves to be victims of their male partners per se; rather they felt like they got something they neither deserved nor anticipated. Consequently, most tried to do something to stop the violence *without* leaving their relationships. This characteristic response is a key element in the gender entrapment of the African American battered women.

In contrast, the white battered women did not experience as much disbelief when the violence began. Being abused, disrespected, and humiliated was part of their previous experiences and was consistent with the white women's sense of themselves and their expectations of adult intimate relationships. They recognized abuse for what it was earlier than the African American battered women did, and they responded to it more quickly and effectively—even if only to accept the abuse and not be as emotionally vulnerable to its consequences.

3. Emotional Work to Manage the Discrepancy

The discrepancy that emerged between the socially and cultur-ally–determined ideals about family life and the African American battered women's reality in their public and private worlds set in motion a pattern of emotional and behavioral responses intended to ease the tension created by the contradictions they felt.[19] Some of the African American battered women denied the tense feelings created by the discrepancy between their reality and the ideal, while others deferred opportunities or made decisions that they knew would limit their options in order to feel more in con-cert with the ideological norm. A few worked emotionally, be-haviorally, and socially to create public identities to disguise their private realities.[20] Most used a combination of these strate-gies to more closely approximate the hegemonic notion of a woman's role in public and private life. This contradiction be-tween dominant ideology, their lived experiences that were in-consistent with this ideology, their hopes for the future, and their ambivalent cultural solidarity with violent men created an ongoing tension for the African American battered women. The tension was an influential and dynamic force in their lives, af-fecting their gender roles in their family, altering their relation-ships with the social world, and influencing their understanding and response to public and private events.

The white women, who did not experience a discrepancy in the same way, turned their energies and efforts to trying to leave the abusive relationships by plotting escapes and in some cases seeking services from public agencies. They were typically less emotionally ambivalent, and they faced more practical concerns, such as how to support themselves and their children alone. This was an important distinction because while the white women had some difficulty gaining services, their abuse was known to others and did not escalate to the horrifying levels that the Af-rican American battered women's did while they were distracted by the discrepancy between their expectations and reality.

4. Social Stigma

Feeling unable to control events in the domestic sphere ulti-mately led to a deep sense of failure and shame for the African American battered women. They described repeated attempts to stop the violence, to manage it more effectively, or to conceal the consequences of the abuse. The amount of energy and resources that went into living with violence in their intimate relationships was enormous, draining them emotionally, spiritually, physically, and materially.

Simultaneously, the African American battered women were feeling the humiliation of public stigma. Their social status, which had increased because of their (assumed) permanent relationships with men, was threatened as the women's dreams became nightmares. The sense of public failure and accompanying loss of social, community, and family status reinforced the private shame and guilt many of the African American battered women felt. Some of their families overtly blamed the women either for the abuse or for not being able to cope with it. Other African American battered women lost their jobs, were unable to adequately care for their children, and some became homeless. Their experiences confirm the research that suggests that in New York City, for example, at least thirty–five percent of women residing in homeless shelters report that they are there because of violence in their intimate relationships, and forty percent of children placed in foster care have mothers who were battered.

Being a battered woman did not carry as much social stigma for the white women. They did not feel as invested in concealing the abuse and protecting the reputation of the abusers or as worried that their images would be tarnished if knowledge of the abuse became public. That the white women felt that they had less to lose was related to the racial/ethnic vulnerability to social stigma that the African American battered women felt. Unlike the white battered women, the African American battered women felt concerned about their community's response to them if they revealed that they were being battered because they were thought to have had such promise. They were also worried about society's potentially negative response to them as African American women if they disclosed negative information about their family lives. The white battered women, being less burdened by social stigma, were more protective of themselves and less affected by the risk of disclosing negative information about their lives.

5. Lack of Services and Isolation

The combined effect of private guilt and public humiliation led the African American battered women in this study to ultimately become very isolated as they attempted to resolve their problems with violence alone. They avoided their families either out of shame or fear for their families' safety, and they tended not to use social services and to avoid criminal justice solutions to the battering. The few who did use public services found them unhelpful. Service providers were unresponsive; they minimized the abuse, and they were insensitive to the cultural nuances and beliefs the women held about their relationships with men. Some African American battered women recounted overtly racist experiences with human–service providers that led them to feel protective of the African American men who abused them.

In addition, the overall lack of crisis–intervention services in low–income communities of color meant that their attempts to reach out for help typically failed and left the African American battered women at greater risk of abuse as long police response time, lack of shelter space, and lack of safe affordable housing exacerbated their vulnerability to abuse. The African American battered women were left socially isolated, physically hurt, and emotionally traumatized, and the violence escalated.

The white battered women tended to know about, to seek, and to utilize services much more readily. While they were also very isolated in terms of social networks, the white women felt more entitled to the use of social services and requested public intervention when they were in crisis. Without overstating the availability of services for the white battered women in this study, when they sought assistance, service providers tended to be more responsive to their plight. The white battered women did not feel as stigmatized or as misunderstood as the African American battered women did, and they were more likely than the African American battered women to have episodic encounters with agencies or programs that were trying to help them.

6. Escalation of the Violence and Increased Vulnerability

Characteristically, the violence escalated over time for both the African American and the white women. However, since the white women were more likely to be connected to public agencies, they were in less danger than the African American battered women, who feared that the physical assaults would kill them. The African American battered women felt that no one would believe the extent and nature of the abuse or that they had not left the relationship, given their historical self–confidence and personal ability. Thus began the downward spiral into more violence, more injury, more shame, more isolation, and more abuse. Even those who fought back did so with ambivalence, knowing that fighting back could escalate the violence.

Contrary to the increasingly popular notion that battered women have masochistic tendencies, all of the battered women in this study despised the violence and wanted it to stop. The distinguishing factor between the two groups of battered women in this study was the *means* they chose to try to accomplish this. None of the African American battered women interviewed for this book wanted their batterer to be arrested and go to jail. Nor did they want their relationships to end. Instead, they described the various ways they worked to control their abusive partners' behavior, far beyond the limits of their abilities. The African American battered women's failure to successfully create safer households represented a serious challenge to their identities and sense of competence in the private sphere, and as their efforts to help themselves failed, the violence got worse. Ultimately, they found themselves isolated and in very dangerous situations, vulnerable to extreme forms of abuse.

In contrast, the white women's experiences did not distinguish the relationship from the violence, and they believed that in order to escape from the violence they would have to leave the men who were abusing them. They had no illusions that their partners would stop the abuse, and felt they would exercise any options they could, including having the batterers arrested. Three of the four white battered women whose stories are told in this book volunteered that they had considered killing their abuser if they had to in order to get away from him. That none of the African American battered women reported that she considered this option indicates how gender entrapment had them engaged in a process of sacrificing themselves rather than "ruining" their batterers' lives.

THE ILLEGAL ACTIVITIES
IN A SOCIAL CONTEXT

The final category in the sequence of events that constitutes gender entrapment for the African American battered women interviewed for this study was the women's participation in illegal activities. A pattern emerged that distinguished the African American battered women from the other two groups in this study and showed them to have resorted to criminal activities in response to violence in their intimate relationships in particular ways.

For the African American battered women, the series of shifts in their identities, the lack of social services and public support, and conflicting emotional states were central factors in their participation in illegal activities. The sense of power that these women experienced as children in their households of origin was threatened over time by their lack of occupational, educational, and economic success as women. The women's longing for respect and a sense of accomplishment that they were led to believe was possible was unfulfilled in the social world. However, they continued to feel that a productive family life was within the reach of their abilities, even with the onset of the initial abuse in their intimate relationships.

As the violence became more severe, the African American battered women realized that even their goal to establish and maintain domestic lives that were consistent with the ideological norm was impossible, despite their constant efforts. The trauma was emotional as well as physical; the African American battered women were very seriously injured, their mobility was restricted and they became very isolated. Most of them were permanently disfigured. Some of the African American battered women were threatened with death if they left the relationships. The research on domestic homicide renders their fear legitimate. Homicide or attempted homicide is a more likely consequence of leaving an abusive situations than staying in one.[21]

Faced with this situation, most of the African American battered women were not only terrified and hurt, they were frustrated and angry at the lack of assistance or recognition that their victimization received from neighbors, social–service workers, and health–care providers. Even though most of the African American battered women did not reach out for help, they paradoxically described feeling particularly abandoned and betrayed by their families, having grown up with extended social–support networks. They resisted turning to the criminal–justice system out of loyalty to African American men, and yet they resented their isolation, their vulnerability, and their sense of powerlessness. It is here that their gender entrapment becomes particularly evident, leaving them in a no–win situation.

It is important to consider the question of the women's agency or choice at this point. Indeed, on the one hand, the women whose stories are told in this book did make decisions at various times about what they would and would not do. To fully understand their choices, one must try to look at the world from their perspective. At the time that they became involved in illegal activity, the African American battered women felt deeply ineffective in and mistrustful of the public sphere. And they felt powerless to change their social position.

At the same time, while they felt incompetent in the private sphere of their lives, they felt that they understood it better. Even as their situation became more dangerous, at least their partner's abuse was predictable. They believed that they knew his wrath and despite the fear, the injury and the humiliation they experienced, this sense of predictability was safer for them than the unknown, especially since the public sphere offered no such predictability or safety. This, coupled with the fact that violent men are more likely to kill a woman that they are battering if she leaves,[22] helps to explain why the women whose stories are told in this book—and countless other battered women—stay in abusive relationships.

Given the broader social conditions that the African American battered women lived in, staying *for them* meant participating in illegal activity. From their perspective—created by their experience of abuse and their marginalized social location—becoming involved in crime was a reasonable behavioral response to abuse—it was a part of their survival strategy. Add to this a consideration of the African American battered women's commitment to the dominant ideology about family life, their adherence to cultural loyalty to African American men and we can see how the convergence of these factors compelled the African American battered women into crime. Their participation in illegal activities takes on a new meaning when analyzed from within this context.

1. Battered Women and Illegal Drug Use

Illegal drugs were readily available in most of the communities where the women detained at Rikers Island lived before they were arrested, and most of their families or social networks had been deeply affected by the recent epidemic of crack cocaine and the resurgence of intravenous heroin use.[23] Several factors distinguished the African American battered women's experiences as gender entrapment from the other two groups arrested on drug-related charges. The first and most significant impression from the interviews was that most of the African American battered women who became addicted to drugs began seriously using them in response to being battered rather than prior to the onset of the abuse. Contrary to the findings from the African American non–battered women who associated drug use with an increase of violence in their lives, the African American battered women tended to believe that using drugs enhanced their safety.[24] For many it was a way to create a sense of intimacy with their violent partners or to avoid a violent episode.

The meaning that consumption or sales of illegal substances assumed for the three groups also distinguished the African American battered women's experiences as gender entrapment. Whereas the African American non–battered women and the white women became involved with illegal drugs for social purposes—as a part of peer relationships or as an economic activity—the African American battered women reported being forced into the consumption of illegal drugs by their partners, some of whom went so far as to inject them with addictive substances against their will.

Experts in the substance–abuse treatment field have established that one of the most devastating aspects of addiction in contemporary society is the rapid decline in economic status and health.[25] All of the women I interviewed who became addicted to drugs eventually turned to selling them or engaged in other illegal activities to support their drug habits, which sometimes cost them as much as $600 a day. For the African American battered women who were forced or coerced into illegal drug activity by the dynamics of gender entrapment, their physical deterioration was hastened by the injuries they sustained. Their gender entrapment was characterized by the vicious cycle of using drugs as an attempt to avoid violence from their batterers, trying to numb their physical and emotional pain through the use of drugs or alcohol, looking for their next fix, and trying to avoid the police.

2. The Relationship between Poverty, Economic Crimes, and Violence Against Women

Eighty percent of all women detained at Rikers Island Correctional Facility were living at or below the poverty level at the time of their arrests. Second to drug–related offenses were economically motivated crimes. Almost all of the women whose stories are told in the previous chapters lived marginally: constantly at risk of unemployment, without economic cushions, often having to provide for their extended families as well as their children.

The economically motivated crimes can be distinguished as products of gender entrapment where the conditions of poverty were accentuated for the African American battered women by their batterers' rigid control of the families' economic resources, even for the women who were the primary wage earners in the households. Unlike the white battered women and the African American non–battered women, the African American battered women typically did not control their illegally obtained earnings or accumulate enough money to open options. Instead, they stole property, forged checks, stole credit cards, or robbed stores in response to their batterers' demands and to avoid their threatening or violent behavior. As such, the economically motivated crimes that the African American battered women committed were consistent with the theory of gender entrapment, whereas the other groups' were not.

3. Violence Against Women and Illegal Sex Work

By some accounts, women's participation in prostitution and other involvement in the illegal sex industry could also be considered economically motivated. Indeed, many women who are excluded from other occupational options support themselves, their families, and other members of their community through occasional or casual sex work. These were not the women who were arrested and detained at Rikers Island on charges of prostitution. Apart from the feminist debate about whether prostitution is a source of women's sexual and economic liberation or not, the African American battered women in this study who were involved in the sex industry were forced into organized prostitution as an extension of their abuse, characterizing their experiences as gender entrapment. Unlike the white battered women and the African American non–battered women who worked more independently in the sex industry, the African American battered women who worked as prostitutes had no control over the money they earned or the conditions of their work. Their batterers selected their customers, the women worked very long hours in dangerous places for very little pay, and were forced to perform or participate in sexual acts of which they were ashamed. The violent men used the fact that the women were prostitutes to discredit them and as a reason to abuse, humiliate, and exploit them, forcing the women into more prostitution and the shameful silence associated with gender entrapment.

4. Assaults and Property Damage by Battered Women

The theory of gender entrapment that links gender–identity development and violence to illegal activity also explains how some African American women were so profoundly affected by the abuse that their reactions to subsequent physical threats were characterized by overreacting with undue force. For some, their efforts to protect themselves when they perceived a threat to their safety could be conceptualized as a flashback, which is documented in the literature as a common feature of post–traumatic stress syndrome.[26] Others were led to commit crimes by a less organized series of thoughts and events when they were reminded of their abusers. In either case, the gender entrapment of some African American battered women in this study took the form of being criminally sanctioned for their involvement in illegal activities that resulted from having been battered for years and left unprotected by criminal, social, and familial systems. When the African American battered women took action to *protect themselves* (as they were socialized to do in their families of origin), they were essentially penalized for not relying on the systems that they felt had failed them in the past.

In contrast, the white women who were arrested for assault or property damage did not attribute their crimes to having been battered. They tended to be emotionally detached from the abuser, to leave the violent relationships, or to receive assistance from an outside agency. As a result, they were not left as vulnerable to prolonged and persistent violence, and their defense could more easily document a legal claim of "self–defense." They were ultimately less vulnerable in their intimate relationships and less likely to be involved in and prosecuted for illegal activities they committed in response to being battered.

5. *Violence Against Women and Child Abuse*

The research on family violence corroborates the fact that children whose mothers are battered are at a much higher risk than other children of abuse from accidental injury, emotional trauma resulting from observing violence, and of being abused themselves by parents.[27] However, contrary to the popular conception that battered women respond to being abused by retaliating against their children, battered women are much less likely to abuse their children than their abusive husbands are. Even though they may not be the primary assailant, it is still difficult for most social scientists, legal theorists, and feminist activists to conceive of how an adult—especially a child's own mother— can observe or know about a child being hurt or killed and not intervene. The social instinct is to hold the adult morally and legally accountable for failing to protect a child without regard for how badly the adult might have been simultaneously hurt. This is particularly true if the adult happens to be the abused child's mother.

Indeed, the stories of the African American battered women who were being detained at Rikers Island for crimes of child endangerment and infanticide were, for me, the most difficult to hear. The analogy of being battered to being held hostage by terrorists, which is made by some experts on violence in intimate relationships, offers a helpful context for understanding how a battered woman could not intervene to save her child's life.[28] In the case of the African American battered women interviewed for this book, child abuse and neglect leading to the murder of a child was caused by male violence and the battered women's inability to protect their children from abusive husbands. This, of all the illegal activity that resulted from violence in intimate relationships, illustrated the most disturbing and indeed the most lethal consequences of gender entrapment.

6. Loyalty and Stereotypes of African American Battered Women

The factors that distinguish the African American battered women's path to illegal activity as gender entrapment are complicated by the issue of socially constructed loyalty to African American men. As the literature on paternalism in the criminal–justice system suggests, in the past ten years there has been a significant shift away from the tendency to arrest, charge, and sentence women with more leniency than male offenders.[29]

Still, most of the African American battered women interviewed for this book believed that if they were arrested they would be treated less harshly by the criminal justice authorities than their male partners or other African American men. Some took the rap for their mutual criminal behavior, using the language of ideology, cultural loyalty, and racial/ethnic solidarity to explain why they were in jail instead of their male partners. Other African American battered women in the sample reported that their male partners threatened them with violence if they did not enter a guilty plea as the primary defendant in their cases. Other abusive African American men set up the battered women so that they would be arrested by leaving them uncovered or by planting illegal drugs or weapons on them, then neglected to post bail. In all these situations, gender and ethnicity became important variables in the gender–entrapment analysis because they affected how the African American battered women presented themselves in the public sphere and how the criminal justice system responded to them and African American men. This finding is particularly important to the gender–entrapment theory in light of the current research on the dynamics of race/ethnicity, gender, and sentencing patterns.

Diane Lewis and other African American feminist criminologists suggest that understanding the experiences of women of color in the criminal justice system requires an examination of how the stereotypes about Black women (e.g., they are more violent, less controllable, and less feminine) contradict the dominant ideology about women's roles (passive, family–based).[30] The gender–entrapment model of women's illegal activities, taken with this body of research, explains how African American battered women come to be incarcerated in this country. As this study of gender entrapment established, some African American battered women were in jail because they lost their eligibility to criminal justice protection and social support when they became involved in illegal activities as an extension of being abused by men who were considered more socially oppressed than they were. They were arrested because they failed in their roles as mothers, were forced to use their sexuality as a commodity, or were seeking comfort, intimacy, or income through illegal drug activity. Some regained a sense of self–protection and declared they'd never let a man touch them again. In any case, their path to crime was complicated by the popular stereotypical image of the strength (hence, lack of feminine attributes) of African American women that erased the possibility in the consciousness of the mainstream public *and* the African American community (and perhaps in their own minds as well) that they could have been as brutally battered as they were.

Being poor complicated the gender entrapment because, like most other women at Rikers Island, the African American battered women interviewed for this book did not have the economic resources to post bail, hire a specialized attorney who could incorporate issues of violence into their defense, or otherwise negotiate the class–biased criminal justice system. In the end, the African American battered women whose stories are told here were vulnerable to abuse because of the public and private conditions of their lives. They committed crimes in response to the abuse, then were penalized for the behaviors that were consistent with their gender identity and their social positions. Their culturally constructed relationships with African American men who were vulnerable to biased criminal–justice practices, among other forms of discrimination, solidified the gender entrapment of the African American battered women.

A COMPARATIVE ANALYSIS OF THE THREE SUB-GROUPS

A clearer understanding of the gender–entrapment paradigm is revealed when the experiences of the African American women who were battered are distinguished from women from the other two groups of incarcerated women I interviewed for this study.

While the research design for this project did not require the use of a random sample or control group, the use of the two comparison groups and a model group, as directed by the principles of theoretical sampling, helped uncover the specific mechanisms of gender entrapment with regard to race/ethnicity and violence.[31] Even though the comparison groups were relatively small, further conclusions about gender entrapment was gleaned from a comparative analysis of the three subgroups that comprised the sample in this study.

The Impact of Violence

A comparison of the African American battered women's gender–identity development to the gender–identity development of the African American women who were not battered showed that both groups were influenced in significant ways by the organization of their households of origin. However, the non–battered women were less affected by the dominant ideology, their families were more isolated from social institutions in the dominant social structure, and they had looser networks of social support in their communities. The African American women who were not battered were less likely to be influenced by hegemonic values than either of the other two groups.

Additionally, the African American women who were not battered expressed less sensitivity to the social and economic position of African American men than the African American battered women did, and they identified more strongly with their mothers and women caretakers as members of an oppressed group. They understood that some African American men abused their experience of racial inequality as an excuse to subordinate African American women, which led them to establish an oppositional stance toward men in their lives. The African American non–battered women grew up expecting to be treated badly by men and were therefore less likely to tolerate or excuse physical abuse.

The one area in which they did express solidarity with African American men was in the distrust of the criminal–justice system. However, since the women were not victimized by men in an ongoing way, they did not need to depend on its agents for protection against them. Ironically, the African American non–battered women identified themselves as "victims of the system" more than "criminal" or "offenders," whereas the African American battered women had a more complex analysis of their multiple identities that had shifted over time.

In terms of the paths that African American non–battered women took to criminal activities, they were much more frequently charged with drug–related offenses (possession and/or sales) or with robbery or burglary than the other groups. As such, they were more like the typical of women detained in correctional institutions across the country. Few of the women in this subgroup expected or imagined paternal criminal justice practices, and hence were not likely to "take the bus" for the men in their lives.

The Effect of Race

Further refinement of the gender–entrapment model that was developed in this study was gained from a comparison between the African American battered women and the experience of the white battered women in the sample. For the white women, gender identity was also constructed in their families of origin; however, even though their families more closely mirrored the ideological norm in structure, they were in fact more dysfunctional. The white battered women's attempts to attain the ideologically normative family structure were characterized by less failure, and therefore created less internal tension and less ambivalence about their rights and privileges as women; however, their families were generally patriarchal, rigid, oppressive environments.

Another significant difference between the white battered women and the African American battered women was the absence of culturally constructed sensitivity to men's needs. The white women felt inferior to the men in their lives from a very early age. Unlike the African American battered women, they did not feel that they had the means, strength, or interest in protecting their men.

In terms of their relationship to the legal system, the white battered women developed mistrust of the criminal justice system *after* being arrested, in contrast to the African American women, who felt mistrustful even *before* their direct involvement. Therefore, the white women used crisis–intervention programs for battered women and law–enforcement services when they were victims of crimes even though they were involved in illegal activities themselves. The white women did not develop a contradictory identity (criminal vs. victim of a crime), as did the other women. They tended to leave the battering relationships sooner and, therefore, suffered less abuse than the African American battered women. The white battered women recognized and understood the patterns of abuse for what they were and, as such, they were less entrapped in violent situations than the African American battered women. The paths that the white women took to criminal activities were also different. They were not held hostage or terrorized in the same way, nor did they attack their batterers or other men who represented their batterers. They were less likely to be arrested for arson, other property damage, or assault of other men because they had external protection and support. Their assaults of their batterers were characterized as self–defense.

7

CONCLUSION

THE WOMEN whose stories are told in this book—
African American battered women who are compelled to crime—
represent a tragic portrayal of life in contemporary society.
Some readers might conclude that their accounts were unusual
in the degree of violence, degradation, and betrayal they experienced. A more careful reading would have hopefully revealed
that the extent to which they were influenced by hegemonic aspirations, the ways they negotiated contradictory influences,
and the deals they cut to survive were tragically common. The
individual stories dramatically portray a regrettable set of everyday circumstances.

Their collective story tells of a complex series of events in the
public sphere and conditions in the private domain of countless
women's lives in contemporary society. Violence by their intimate partners created chaos in their lives—acute injury, chronic
pain, sexual degradation, and emotional trauma. Racism furthered the impact of violence and influenced the sense of loyalty
to the men who battered them and adherence to the cultural values regarding gender roles and relationships. Poverty seriously
limited the options the African American women felt in response to the intimate and systemic abuse. Their economic con-

dition made the stigma and shame worse, and, in some instances, led them to choose the survival strategies that furthered the impact of social marginalization. This, combined with their aspirations of success, their invisibility to human service programs, and more aggressive criminal justice policies compelled the African American battered women to crime. Their involvement in the illegal activities that led to their arrest and detention in Rikers Island Correctional Facility is the story of gender entrapment that is told in this book.

Two obvious questions emerge from this research: "How could the African American battered women's lives have been different?" and "What is the solution to gender entrapment?" As this study was designed to develop the theoretical model, the answers are appropriately linked to further research that would include: 1) attempting to develop a standardized instrument to measure gender entrapment, and 2) testing the theoretical model with other populations. However, at this time, these concluding questions serve a more rhetorical purpose: to highlight three policy issues that are raised by the gender–entrapment model.

THE STIGMA OF DEVIANCE

First, the findings from this study point to the ways that gender, race/ethnicity, and violence interact with social stigma and deviance to negatively affect some social actors' life histories. In this sample, the women who experienced gender entrapment had six stigmatized identities. In the most general sense, they were marginalized as *women* in a patriarchal society. Second, as *African American* women, their identities were influenced by ethnic stigma and discriminatory treatment arising from prejudice, stereotypes, and institutionalized racism. As *low income* women, the third source of social stigma, they did not have access to the means by which they could reach the hegemonic state of "appropriate womanhood" or "good parent." The stigma of being *battered women* symbolized their failure to accomplish the socially constructed expectations and desires for safety and comfort in their domestic spheres. When the women became *criminals*, they violated still another normative standard based on the assumption of obedience and morality. This was especially significant in those cases where the women's crimes were associated with their roles as mothers or sexual actors. Finally, as *incarcerated* women, they broke the last taboo and experienced the stigma of being arrested, charged, and detained in a correctional facility for socially deviant behaviors and/or illegal activities.

The African American battered women who are in jails for crimes that resulted from gender entrapment are among the most stigmatized group in contemporary society. While the emotional effects of their stigmatized identities and the consequences of their deviant behavior may represent mental health or rehabilitative concerns, the *root causes* of the stigma they experience and its relationship to social variables raise important sociological questions. The policy implications surround developing strategies to interrupt the social, economic, and political forces that lead to "deviance," to mediate the long–term effects of stigma based on gender, ethnicity, and the experience of violence, and to reverse the social trends outlined in Chapter One.

THE LEGAL IMPLICATIONS
OF THE QUESTION OF AGENCY

In this study, I attempted to explain how women's behaviors are influenced by dynamic and dichotomous forces—historical circumstances *and* contemporary social conditions, events in the public *and* private spheres, and conscious *and* unconscious processes. As an alternative explanation of women's involvement in crime, I offer the theoretical model of gender entrapment, which is based on the understanding that some women are "lured into compromising acts." My model necessarily raises the legal questions of intentionality and duress. From a philosophical perspective, the questions include: "What are the limits of free will and individual choice?" and "In what ways did the African American battered women in this study lack or exercise agency?" As the stories in the preceding chapters show, for some women, involvement in illegal activities could be considered an exercise of their agency, and it may be possible to interpret their crimes in terms that would limit their culpability. This policy issue suggests the need for further analysis of gender entrapment from the perspective of feminist legal scholarship in order to explore the utility of the model in the defense of some battered women who commit crimes, especially those whose experiences and profiles fall outside the dominant theoretical and legal paradigms.

THE RELATIONSHIP BETWEEN THE PLIGHT
OF AFRICAN AMERICAN MEN AND BATTERED
AFRICAN AMERICAN WOMEN

The third issue that the gender–entrapment theoretical model raises is related to the current debate concerning the plight of Black men in contemporary society. The debate focuses on issues such as the skyrocketing incarceration and homicide rates, the troubling unemployment statistics, and the highly publicized cases of police brutality directed toward African American men. These issues are of legitimate sociological and political concern, reflecting a larger economic crisis that is disproportionately affecting the African American community, resulting in a sense of collective devastation and individual despair. Unfortunately, in some instances, the alienation and hopelessness have led to aggression and violence turned inward. This response and the underlying causes of the crisis situation in the African American community require critical attention, policy reform ,and the immediate infusion of resources.

It has been my experience, however, that the framework for the analysis and the construction of the responses to the crisis is seriously flawed in its oversight of the relationship between the erosion of community services, racism, and gender inequality. This oversight not only renders African American women's experiences invisible or insignificant, but has led to the questions being posed in such a way as to position African American women as one of the sources of African American men's oppression.

At the very least, I hope that the women's stories in this book will *not* be used superficially by social scientists to further the anti–Black–male sentiment in contemporary society. Instead, my hope is that the gender–entrapment theoretical model will expand the terms of the debate and deepen the analysis to include a critical feminist perspective on the particular ways that gender inequality affects African American women in relation to African American men *as well as* how institutionalized sexism and racism have severely limited the lives of African American people in contemporary society.

This reframing of the issues in order to broaden the context of the debate requires both a qualitative as well as quantitative assessment of the social circumstances of African American men and women, and a comparative analysis by gender. Public policies and social programs must not reproduce gender inequality as a strategy to decrease African American men's social, economic, and political inequality, but must take seriously the needs of African American women and girls as well as African American men and boys. For example, educational interventions, community services, and political organizing must not only include African American women and girls as clients or participants, but must address the ways that, despite their oppressed status, individual African American men's behavior may indeed be abusive toward women, and how social institutions, including those in the African American community, are dominated by men. The empirical, epistemological, and concrete outcomes of this broader project, therefore, must take into account the *intersectionality* of race, class, and gender oppression, as this study of gender entrapment attempted to do.[1]

THE NEED FOR SOCIAL CHANGE

It could be said that this study of gender entrapment described the most extreme negative consequences when gender inequality, economic marginalization, violence against women, biased criminal justice practices, and racism intersect. The African American battered women whose lives served as the empirical basis for development of this theoretical model represent not only the loss of comfort, productive potential, and opportunity for self–determination, but indeed the loss of life that results from the combination of gender violence, social inequality, and crime. Had the dynamics between the circumstances in the public and the private sphere of their lives been different, some of the African American battered women in this study might have been extraordinarily successful. Their strength, self–confidence, cultural and family loyalty, and the optimism that ultimately led to gender entrapment were potentially their greatest assets. Instead of positioning them for success, the convergence of their experiences in the public and private spheres left them vulnerable to social marginalization, violence in their intimate relationships, and ultimately to incarceration for crimes they committed in response to their gender entrapment.

My hope is that the women's stories in this book will be dignified by the treatment of the theory of gender entrapment I have developed. I hope that their lives will be better understood and

that the debate about the deadly consequences of institutionalized racism will include a gendered analysis. I also hope that I
have been able to make theoretical and methodological contributions to a body of feminist scholarship that privileges the voices
of those most overlooked and misrepresented by the current discourse. Should the effects of violence, marginalization, racism
and culturally constructed gender roles be taken more seriously
by those who determine the outcomes of battered women's legal
cases, then the telling of their stories will have made a difference. And finally, I hope that women in the future have many
more options than the women whose stories are told in this
book, so that fewer African American women will be battered
and incarcerated because of gender entrapment.

NOTES

CHAPTER I / INTRODUCTION

1. hooks, bell in *Double Stitch: Black Women Write about Mothers and Daughters*, pp. 149–150. Edited by Patricia Bell Scott and Beverly Guy Sheffar, 1991, Beacon Press.

2. Statistics in this paragraph are quoted from: American Correctional Association, 1990. *The Female Offender: What Does the Future Hold?* (Washington, D.C. St. Mary's Press.)

3. 1995 New York City Department of Corrections Population Data. 1990. U.S. Department of Justice, Office of Justice Programs in Bureau of Justice Statistics Bulletin: "Jail and Jail Inmates 1993–94."

4. Phyllis J. Baunach, *Mothers in Prison* (New Brunswick: Transition Books, 1988), and Seetta Moss, "Women in Prison: A Case of Pervasive Neglect," *Women in Therapy* (1986) 5:2–3, 177–185. Emerson Dobash and Russell P. Dobash, *Women, Violence and Social Change* (New York: Routledge, 1992). Patricia Hill Collins, *Black Feminist Thought: Knowledge, Consciousness and the Politics of Empowerment* (Boston: Unwin Hyman, 1990).

5. Patricia Hill Collins, *Black Feminist Thought*.

6. Leslie Brody, "Gender Differences in Emotional Development: A Review of Theories and Research." In *Gender and Personality: Current Perspectives on Theory and Research*, ed. A. J. Stewart and M. B. Lykes (Durham: Duke University, 1985). Allison Jagger, "Love and Knowledge:

Emotion in Feminist Epistemology," *Gender/Body/Knowledge: Feminist Reconstruction of Being and Knowing*, ed. A. Jagger and S. Bordo (New Brunswick: Rutgers University).

7. Susan Schechter, *Women and Male Violence: The Visions and Struggles of the Battered Women's Movement* (Boston: South End Press, 1982).

8. R. Emerson Dobash and Russell P. Dobash, *Women, Violence and Social Change*. Murray A. Straus and Richard J. Gelles, "Societal Change and Change in Family Violence from 1975 to 1985 as Revealed by Two National Surveys," *Journal of Marriage and the Family* (1986) 48:465–479.

9. W. Hudson and S. McIntosh, "The Assessment of Spouse Abuse: Two Quantifiable Dimensions," *Journal of Marriage and the Family* (1981) 43:873–885. Murray Arnold Straus and Richard J. Gelles, *Physical Violence in American Families: Risk Factors and Adaptations to Violence in 8,145 Families* (New Brunswick: Transition Publications, 1990). Lewis Okun, *Women abuse: Facts Replacing Myths* (Albany: State University Press, 1986).

10. Kristin Yllo and Michele Bograd, "Political Methodological Debates in Wife Abuse Research," *Feminist Perspectives on Wife Abuse*, ed. K. Yllo and M. Bograd (Newbury Park: Sage, 1988).

11. *Violence in the Black Family: Correlates and Consequences*, ed. Robert Hampton (Lexington, Mass.: Lexington Books, 1987).

12. Gondolf, Edward W., Muley, Edward, P. and Lidz, Charles W. 1990. "Characteristics of Perpetrators of Family and Non–Family Assaults." *Hospital and Community Psychiatry*, February, Volume 41(2) 191–193.

13. *The Speaking Profits Us: Violence in the Lives of Women of Color*, ed. Mary Violet C. Burns (Seattle: The Center for the Prevention of Sexual and Domestic Violence, 1986). Kanuha, Valli. "Race and Spouse Abuse: A Social Constructionist's Analysis of Battering," in Edelson, Jeff and Eisikovits, Zvi, *The Future of Intervention with Battered Women and their Children* (Beverly Hills: Sage Publication, 1995.)

14. Evelina Giobbe, "Coalition Against Trafficking in Women Proposes United Nations Convention on Sexual Exploitation," *Women Hurt in Systems of Prostitution Engaged in Revolt Newsletter* (1992), 4:1–2.

15. National Commission on Crime and Delinquency, *Focus* (December 1989), 1.

16. National Commission on Acquired Immune Deficiency Syndrome, *Executive Summary: America Living with AIDS* (Washington, D.C., 1991). Committee for Substance Abuse Coverage Study, Division of Health Care Services, Institute of Medicine, *Treating Drug Problems*,

Volume 1, ed. Dean Gerstein and Henrick Harwood. (Washington, D.C.: National Academy Press, 1990).

17. John Irwin, *The Jail: Managing the Underclass in American Society* (Berkeley: University of California, 1985).

18. New York State Coalition Against Domestic Violence, "Domestic Violence Hearings Held at Bedford Hills Correctional Facility," *NYSCADV Newsletter* (April 1985).

CHAPTER 2 / LIFE HISTORIES

1. Catherine Marshall and Gretchen Rossman, *Designing Qualitative Research* (Newbury Park: Sage, 1989).

2. Elliot George Mishler, *Research Interviewing: Context and Narrative* (Cambridge: Harvard University, 1986). Lawrence Watson and Maria–Barbara Watson–Franke, *Interpreting Life Histories* (New Brunswick: Rutgers University, 1985).

3. Joye Ladner, *Tomorrow's Tomorrow: The Black Woman* (New York: Doubleday, 1972). See page 81.

4. Sandra Harding, "Is There a Feminist Method?" *Feminism and Methodology: Social Science Issues*, ed. S. Harding (Bloomington: Indiana University, 1987).

5. Dorothy E. Smith, *The Everyday World as Problematic: A Feminist Sociology* (Boston: Northeastern University, 1987).

6. Howard Schwartz and Jerry Jacobs, *Qualitative Sociology: A Method to the Madness* (New York: The Free Press, 1979). Patricia Maguire, *Doing Participatory Research: A Feminist Approach* (Amherst: The Center for International Education, University of Massachusetts, 1987). Eleanor Miller, *Street Women* (Philadelphia: Temple University, 1986). Sandra Harding, "Is There a Feminist Method?" Lynn Cannon, Elizabeth Higginbotham and Marianne Leung, "Race and Class Bias in Qualitative Research on Women," *Gender and Society* (1987) 4:449–469.

7. Murray A. Straus and Richard J. Gelles, *Physical Violence in American Families*.

8. I am indebted to Judith Lorber for this idea.

9. Anselm L. Strauss, *Qualitative Analysis for Social Scientists* (San Francisco: University of California, 1990).

10. Federal Bureau of Investigation, *Uniform Crime Reports for the United States* (Washington, D.C.: United States Department of Justice, 1989).

11. Anselm L. Strauss, *Qualitative Analysis for Social Scientists* (San Francisco: University of California, 1990).

12. In ninety–five percent of cases, men are the coercing partners, and women are their victims.

13. M.A. Straus and R.J. Gelles, *Physical Violence in American Fam-*

ilies.

14. Barney G. Glaser and Anselm L. Strauss, *Discovery of Grounded Theory: Strategies for Qualitative Research* (Chicago: Aldine, 1967).

15. M.A. Straus and R.J. Gelles, *Physical Violence in American Families.* See page 43.

16. A Strauss, *Qualitative Analysis for Social Scientists.*

17. Steven Taylor and Robert Bogdan, *Introduction to Qualitative Research* (New York: Wiley, 1984).

18. C. Marshall and G. Rossman, *Designing Qualitative Research.*

19. A. Strauss, *Qualitative Analysis for Social Scientists.*

20. Ileana Arias and Steven Beach, "Validity of Self Reports of Marital Violence," *Journal of Family Violence* (1987) 2(2):139–149.

CHAPTER 3 / GENDER IDENTITY DEVELOPMENT

1. Leith Mullings, "Anthropological Perspective on the Afro–American Family," *American Journal of Psychiatry* (1986) 6:1, 11–16.

CHAPTER 6 / THE STORY OF GENDER ENTRAPMENT

1. Nancy Chodorow, *The Reproduction of Mothering: Psychoanalysis and the Sociology of Gender* (Berkeley: University of California Press, 1978).

2. Niara Sudarkasa, "African Heritage in Afro–American Family Organization," *Black Families*, ed. H.P. McAdoo (Beverly Hills: Sage, 1981).

3. Arlie Hochschild, *The Second Shift: Working Parents and the Revolution at Home* (New York: Viking, 1989).

4. Soraya M. Coley and Joyce O. Beckett, "Black Battered Women: A Review of the Empirical Literature," *Journal of Counseling and Development* (1988) 66:266–276.

5. N. Sudarkasa, "African Heritage."

6. Bonnie Thornton Dill, "Our Mother's Grief: Racial Ethnic Women and the Maintenance of Families," *Journal of Family History* (1988) 13:415–431.

7. National Research Council, *A Common Destiny: Blacks and American Society* (Washington, D.C.: National Academy Press, 1989).

8. Karen Dugger, "Social Location and Gender Role Attitudes: A Comparison of Black and White Women," *Gender and Society* (1988) 2(4):425–448.

9. William Julius Wilson, *The Truly Disadvantaged: The Inner City, The Underclass and Public Policy* (Chicago: University of Chicago, 1987).

10. Linda J. Myers, *Understanding an Afrocentric World View* (Dubuque, Iowa: Kendall Hunt, 1988).

11. Julie Blackman, *Intimate Violence: A Study of Injustice* (New

York: Columbia University, 1989).

12. Evan Stark, Ann Flitcraft, and William Frazier, "Medicine and Patriarchal Violence: The Social Construction of a 'Private Event,'" *International Journal of Health Services* (1977) 9(3):461–494.

13. Jacquelyn Campbell, "Assessment of Patterns of Dangerousness with Battered Women," *Issues in Mental Health Nursing* (1989) 10:245–260.

14. A. Hochschild, *The Second Shift*. Candace West and Don Zimmerman, "Doing Gender," *Gender and Society* (1987) 1:2, 125–151.

15. A. Hochschild, *The Second Shift*.

16. Karen Dugger, "Social Location and Gender Role Attitudes."

17. Angela Browne, *When Battered Women Kill* (New York: The Free Press, 1987).

18. Lenore Walker, *Terrifying Love: Why Battered Women Kill and How Society Responds* (New York: Harper & Row, 1989).

19. Drew Westen, *Self and Society: Narcissism, Collectivism and the Development of Morals* (New York: Cambridge University, 1985).

20. Erving Goffman, *The Presentation of Self in Everyday Life* (New York: Doubleday, 1959.

21. Barbara Hart, "Beyond the 'Duty to Warn': A Therapist's 'Duty to Protect' Battered Women and Children," in *Feminist Perspectives on Wife Abuse*, ed. K. Yllo and M. Bograd (Newbury Park: Sage, 1988).

22. L. Walker, *Terrifying Love*.

23. Marsha Rosenbaum, *Women on Heroin* (New Brunswick: Rutgers University, 1981). Harlow, C.S. "Drugs and Jail/Inmates 1989," Bureau of Justice Statistics Special Report, 1991.

24. Barry Spunt, Paul J. Golstein, Patricia A. Bellucci, and Thomas Miller, "Race/Ethnicity and Gender Differences in the Drugs–Violence Relationship," *Journal of Psychoactive Drugs* (1990) 22:3, 293–303.

25. Douglas Shenson, Nancy Dubler and David Michaels, "Jails and Prisons: The New Asylums?" *American Journal of Public Health* (1990) 80:655–656.

26. Teresa Krammer and Bonnie Green, "Post Traumatic Stress Disorders and Early Response to Sexual Abuse," *Journal of Interpersonal Violence* (1991) 6:2.

27. Bower 1988. Gelles, Richard and Straus, Murray 1987,. "Is Violence Against Children Increasing? A Comparison of 1975 and 1985 National Rates." *Journal of Interpersonal Violence* 2:212–222. Sheridan, M.J. 1994, March, "The Interplay of Parental Substance Abuse and Family Dynamics: Relationship to Abuse and Neglect. Paper presented at the 40th annual program meeting of Committee Social Work Education. Atlanta, Georgia.

28. Graham 1988. Krammer, Teresa L. and Bonnie Green, "Post Traumatic Stress Disorders and Early Response to Sexual Abuse."

29. Keith Crew, "Sex Differences in Criminal Sentencing: Chivalry or Patriarch," *Justice Quarterly* (1991) 8:1, 59–82.

30. Diane Lewis, "Black Women Offenders and Criminal Justice: Some Theoretical Considerations," *Comparing Male and Female Offenders*, ed. M. Warren (Beverly Hills: Sage, 1981).

31. A.L. Strauss, *Qualitative Analysis for Social Scientists* (San Francisco: University of California, 1990).

CHAPTER 7 / CONCLUSION

1. This concept has been developed and utilized by legal scholar Kimberlé W. Crenshaw. Crenshaw, Kimberlé W. 1991. "Demarginalizing the Intersection of Race and Sex: A Black Feminist Critique of Antidiscrimination Doctrine, Feminist Theory, and Antiracist Politics." in *Feminist Legal Theory* 57, 57-58 edited by Katherine T. Bartlett and Rosanne Kennedy.

REFERENCES

Adler, Freda. 1975. *Sisters in Crime: The Rise of the New Female Criminal.* New York: McGraw Hill.

Arias, Ileana and Steven Beach. 1987. "Validity of Self Reports of Marital Violence." *Journal of Family Violence* 2(2) 139-149.

Armon-Jones, Clair. 1986. "The Social Functions of Emotions." In *The Social Construction of Emotions*, edited by R. Harre. New York: Blackwell.

Ashbury, J. 1987. "African American Women in Violent Relationships: An Exploration of Cultural Differences." In *Violence in the Black Family: Correlates and Consequences*, edited by R. Harre. Lexington, MA: Lexington Books.

Attorney General's Task Force on Family Violence. 1984. *Report of the Attorney General's Task Force on Family Violence.* Washington, DC: U.S. Department of Justice.

Baca Zinn, Maxine. 1990. "Family, Feminism and Race in America." *Gender and Society.* 4:68-82.

Baunach, Phyllis J. 1988. *Mothers in Prison.* New Brunswick: Transaction Books.

Benjamin, Jessica. 1988. *The Bonds of Love: Psychoanalysis, Feminism and the Problem of Domination.* New York: Pantheon.

Bickle, Gayle and Ruth Peterson. 1991. "The Impact of Gender Based Family Roles on Criminal Sentencing." *Social Problems.* 38:372-94.

Blackman, Julie. 1989. *Intimate Violence: A Study of Injustice.* New York: Columbia University.

Boyd-Franklin, Nancy. 1983. "Black Life Styles: A Lesson in Survival." In *Class, Race and Sex: The Dynamics of Control,* edited by A. Swerdlow and H. Lessinger. Boston: G.K. Hall.

Brody, Leslie. 1985. "Gender Differences in Emotional Development: A Review of Theories and Research." In *Gender and Personality: Current Perspectives on Theory and Research,* edited by A.J. Stewart and M.B. Lykes. Durham: Duke University.

Browne, Angela. 1987. *When Battered Women Kill.* New York: The Free Press.

Bunch, Barbara, L. Fooley and S. Urbina. 1983. "The Psychology of Violent Female Offenders: A Sex Role Perspective." *The Prison Journal.* 63:2.

Burns, Mary Violet C. (ed). 1986. *The Speaking Profits Us: Violence in the Lives of Women of Color.* Seattle: The Center for the Prevention of Sexual and Domestic Violence.

Campbell, Jacquelyn. 1989. "Assessment of Patterns of Dangerousness with Battered Women." *Issues in Mental Health Nursing.* 10:245-260.

Cancian, Francesca. 1987. *Love in America: Gender and Self-Development.* New York: Cambridge University.

Cannon, Lynn, Elizabeth Higginbotham and Marianne Leung. 1987. "Race and Class Bias in Qualitative Research on Women." *Gender and Society.* 4:449-469.

Chodorow, Nancy. 1978. *The Reproduction of Mothering: Psychoanalysis and the Sociology of Gender.* Berkeley: University of California Press.

Climent, Carlos E., Ann Rollins, Frank R. Ervin, and Robert Plutchik. 1973. "Epidemiological Studies of Women Prisoners: Medical and Psychiatric Variables Related to Violent Behavior." *American Journal of Psychiatry.* 130(9):985-990.

Cochrane, Raymond. 1974. "Values as Correlates of Deviancy." *British Journal of Social and Clinical Psychology.* 13(3):257-267.

Coley, Soraya M. and Joyce O. Beckett. 1988. "Black Battered Women: A Review of the Empirical Literature." *Journal of Counseling and Development.* 66:266-276.

Collins, Patricia Hill. 1986. "Learning from the Outsider Within: The Sociological Significance of Black Feminist Thought." *Social Problems.* 33:514-532.

Collins, Patricia Hill. 1989. "A Comparison of Two Works on Black Family Life." *Signs* 14:875-84.

Collins, Patricia Hill. 1990. *Black Feminist Thought: Knowledge, Consciousness and the Politics of Empowerment.* Boston: Unwin Hyman.

Correctional Association of New York. 1991. *The CA Reporter.* April.

Crenshaw, Kimberlé W. 1991. "Demarginalizing the Intersection of Race and Sex: A Black Feminist Critique of Antidiscrimination Doctrine, Feminist Theory, and Antiracist Politics," in *Feminist Legal Theory* 57, 57-58, eds Katherine T. Bartlett and Rosanne Kennedy.

Crew, Keith B. 1991. "Sex Differences in Criminal Sentencing: Chivalry or Patriarchy." *Justice Quarterly.* 8:1, 59-82.

Currie, Elliot. 1985. *Confronting Crime: An American Challenge.* New York: Pantheon.

Davidoff-Kroop, Joy. 1981. *The Forgotten Offender.* Albany: New York State Program Evaluation and Planning Unit, New York State Division of Parole.

Davis, Angela. 1981. *Women, Race and Class.* New York: Random House.

Dill, Bonnie Thornton. 1988. "Our Mother's Grief: Racial Ethnic Women and the Maintenance of Families." *Journal of Family History.* 13:415-431.

Dobash, R. Emerson and Russell P. Dobash. 19992. *Women, Violence and Social Change.* New York: Routledge.

Drugger, Karen. 1988. "Social Location and Gender Role Attitudes: A Comparison of Black and White Women." *Gender and Society.* 2(4):425-48.

Dubois, Ellen and Vicki Ruiz. 1990. *Unequal Sisters: A Multicultural Reader in U.S. Women's History.* New York: Routledge.

174   References

Emerge. 1991. *Structuring Counseling Programs for Men Who Batter*. Boston: The Emerge Collection.

Engels, Friedrich. 1942. *The Origin of Family, Private Property and the State, in the Light of the Researches of Lewis H. Morgan*. New York: International Publishers.

Federal Bureau of Investigation. 1989. *Uniform Crime Reports for the United States*. Washington, DC: United States Department of Justice.

Franks, David and Shelley Ottenbrite. 1989. *Syllabi and Instructional Material for the Sociology of Emotions*. Washington, DC: The American Sociological Association.

Frazier, E. Franklin. 1966. *The Negro Family in the United States*. Chicago: University of Chicago.

Freely, Malcolm. 1979. *The Process Is Punishment*. New York: Russell Sage.

Gerstein, Dean and Henrick Harwood, eds., 1990. Committee for Substance Abuse Coverage Study, Division of Health Care Services, Institute of Medicine. *Treating Drug Problems*, Volume 1. Washington DC: National Academy Press.

Geertz, C. 1984. "From the Native's Point of View: On the Nature of Anthropological Understanding." In *Cultural Theory: Essays on Mind, Self and Emotion*, edited by R. Schweder and R. Levine. Boston: Cambridge University.

Giobbe, Evelina. 1992. "Coalition Against Trafficking in Women Proposes United Nations Convention on Sexual Exploitation." In *Women Hurt in Systems of Prostitution Engaged in Revolt Newsletter*. 4:1-2.

Glaser, Barney G. and Anselm L. Strauss. 1967. *Discovery of Grounded Theory: Strategies for Qualitative Research*. Chicago: Aldine.

Goffman, Erving. 1959. *The Presentation of Self in Everyday Life*. New York: Doubleday.

Goffman, Erving. 1961. *Asylums: Essays on the Social Situation of Mental Patients and Other Inmates*. Garde City: Anchor Books.

Goffman, Erving. 1986. *Stigma: Notes on the Management of Spoiled Identity*. New York: Simon & Schuster.

Goode, William. 1964. *The Family*. Englewood Cliffs: Prentice Hall.

Greenfield, Laurence A. and Stephanie Minor-Harper. 1991. *Women in Prison*. Washington, DC: U.S. Department of Justice.

Gutman, Herbert. 1976. *The Black Family in Slavery and Freedom: 1750-1925*. Lexington, MA: Lexington Books.

Hampton, Robert (ed). 1987. *Violence in the Black Family: Correlations and Consequences*. Lexington, MA: Lexington Books.

Harding, Sandra. 1987. "Is There a Feminist Method?" in *Feminism and Methodology: Social Science Issues*, edited by S. Harding. Bloomington: Indiana University.

Harre, Rom. 1986. "An Outline of the Social Constructionists Viewpoint," in *The Social Construction of Emotion*, edited by New York: Blackwell.

Hart, Barbara. 1988. "Beyond the 'Duty to Warn': A Therapist's 'Duty to Protect' Battered Women and Children." In *Feminist Perspectives on Wife Abuse*, edited by K. Yllo and M. Bograd. Newbury Park: Sage.

Hochschild, Arlie. 1983. *The Managed Heart: Commercialization of Feeling*. Berkeley: University of California.

Hochschild, Arlie. 1989. *The Second Shift: Working Parents and the Revolution at Home*. New York: Viking.

hooks, bell. 1981. *Ain't I A Woman: Black Women and Feminism*. Boston: South End Press.

Hudson, W. and S. McIntosh. 1981. "The Assessment of Spouse Abuse: Two Quantifiable Dimensions." *Journal of Marriage and the Family*. 43:873-85.

Hunt, Jennifer C. 1989. *The Jail: Managing the Underclass in American Society*. Berkeley: University of California.

Jagger, Allison. 1989. "Love and Knowledge: Emotion in Feminist Epistemology." In *Gender/Body/Knowledge: Feminist Reconstruction of Being and Knowing*, edited by A. Jagger and S. Bordo. New Brunswick: Rutgers University.

Jones, Jacqueline. 1985. *Labor of Love, Labor of Sorrow: Black Women, Work and the Family from Slavery to the Present*. New York: Basic Books.

Kelly, Liz. 1988. *Surviving Sexual Violence*. Minneapolis: University of Minneapolis.

Kemper, Theodore. 1981. "Social Constructionist and Positivist Approach to the Sociology of Emotions." *American Journal of Sociology.* 87:336-62.

Kemper, Theodore. 1990. *Research Agendas in the Sociology of Emotions.* Albany, State University of New York.

Kempinen, Cynthia. 1983. "Changes in the Sentencing Pattern of Male and Female Criminal Defendants." *Prison Journal.* 83:2.

Klein, Dorie. 1973. "The Etiology of Female Crime: A Review of the Literature." *Issues in Criminology.* 8(2):3-30.

Konner, Melvin. 1982. *The Tangled Vine: Biological Constraints on the Human Spirit.* New York: Holt, Rinehart and Winston.

Krammer, Teresa L. and Bonnie Green. 1991. "Post Traumatic Stress Disorder and Early Response to Sexual Abuse." *Journal of Interpersonal Violence.* 6:2.

Ladner, Joyce. 1972. *Tomorrow's Tomorrow: The Black Woman.* New York: Doubleday.

Laslett, Barbara and Johanna Brenner. 1989. "Gender and Social Reproduction: Historical Perspectives." *Annual Review of Sociology.* 15:381-404.

Leonard, Eileen. 1982. *Women, Crime and Society: A Critique of Theoretical Criminology.* New York: Longman, Inc.

Lewis, Diane. 1981. "Black Women Offenders and Criminal Justice: Some Theoretical Considerations." In *Comparing Male and Female Offenders,* edited by M. Warren. Beverly Hills: Sage.

Lewis, Diane. 1990. "A Response to Inequality: Black Women, Racism and Sexism." In *Black Women in America: Social Science Perspectives,* edited by Malson, et al. Chicago: University of Chicago.

Liebow, Elliott. 1967. *Tally's Corner: A Study of Streetcorner Men.* Boston: Little Brown.

Lincoln, Yvonna and Egon Guba. 1985. *Naturalistic Inquiry.* Beverly Hills: Sage.

Lockhart, Lettie L. 1985. "Methodological Issues in Comparative Racial Analyses: The Case of Wife Abuse." *Social Work Research and Abstracts.* 21(2):35-41.

Lutz, C. 1987. "Emotion, Thought and Estrangement: Emotions

as a Cultural Category." *Cultural Anthropology.*

McDermott, M. Joan. 1986. *Female Offenders in New York Stage.* Albany: New York State Division of Criminal Justice Services.

Maguire, Patricia. 1987. *Doing Participatory Research: A Feminist Approach.* Amherst: The Center for International Education, University of Massachusetts.

Marable, Manning. 1983. *How Capitalism Underdeveloped Black America.* Boston: South End Press.

Marshall, Catherine and Gretchen Rossman. 1989. *Designing Qualitative Research.* Newbury Park: Sage.

Martin, Del. 1976. *Battered Wives.* San Francisco: Glide Publications.

Mathis, Arthur. 1978. "Contrasting Approaches to the Study of Black Families." *Journal of Marriage and the Family.* 40:4, 667-76.

Mead, George Herbert. 1962. *Mind, Self and Society. From the Standpoint of the Social Behaviorist.* Chicago: University of Chicago.

Merton, Robert K., Marjorie Fiske and Patricia L. Kendell. 1956. *The Focus Interview: A Manual of Problems and Procedures.* New York: The Free Press.

Miller, Eleanor. 1986. *Street Women.* Philadelphia: Temple University.

Mills, C. Wright. 1951. *White Collar: The American Middle Classes.* New York: Oxford University.

Mishler, Elliot George. 1986. *Research Interviewing: Context and Narrative.* Cambridge: Harvard University.

Morris, Virginia. 1989. "Book Review on *Women, Crime and Criminal Justice* by Allison Morris, and *Female Crime* by Ngarie Naffine. *Women and Criminal Justice.* 1:1.

Morton, Patricia. 1991. *Disfigured Images: The Historical Assault on African American Women.* New York: Greenwood.

Moss, Seetta. 1986. "Women in Prison: A Case of Pervasive Neglect." *Women in Therapy.* 5:2-3, 177-185.

Moynihan, Daniel Patrick. 1981. *The Negro Family: The Case for National Action.* Washington, DC: U.S. Department of Labor,

Office Policy Planning Research.

Mullings, Leith. 1986. "Anthropological Perspectives on the Afro-American Family." *American Journal of Social Psychiatry*, 6:1, 11-16.

Myers, Linda J. 1988. *Understanding an Afrocentric World View.* Dubuque, Iowa: Kendall Hunt.

National Coalition Against Domestic Violence. 1991. "NCADV Statistics." Organizational Fact Sheet.

National Commission on Acquired Immune Deficiency Syndrome. 1991. *Executive Summary: America Living with AIDS.* Washington, DC: National Commission on AIDS.

National Commission on Crime and Delinquency. 1989. *Focus.* December, 1.

National Research Council. 1989. *A Common Destiny: Blacks and American Society.* Washington, DC: National Academy Press.

New York State Coalition Against Domestic Violence. 1985. "Domestic Violence Hearings Held at Bedford Hills Correctional Facility." *NYSCADV Newsletter.* April.

New York State Division of Criminal Justice Services. 1990. *Annual Report.* Albany: New York State Division of Criminal Justice Services.

NiCarthy, Ginny. 1987. *The Ones Who Got Away: Women Who Left Abusive Partners.* Seattle: The Seal Press.

Nobles, Wade. 1978. "Toward an Empirical and Theoretical Framework for Defining Black Families." *Journal of Marriage and the Family.* 40:679-88.

Okun, Lewis, 1986. *Women Abuse: Facts Replacing Myths.* Albany: State University Press.

Osthoff, Susan. 1990. Personal Communication. National Clearinghouse for Defense of Battered Women.

Parsons, Talcott and Robert F. Bales. 1955. *Family: Socialization and Interaction Process.* Glencoe, Ill: The Free Press.

Parsons, Talcott. 1968. "The Position of Identity in the General Theory of Action." In *The Self in Social Interaction*, edited by C. Gordon and K. Gergen. New York: Wiley.

Parsons, Talcott. 1970. "Social Structure and the Development of Personality: Freud's Contribution to the Integration of Psychology and Sociology." In *Personality and Social Systems*, edited by N. Smelser. New York: Wiley.

Patton, Michael Quinn. 1990. *Qualitative Evaluation and Research Methods*. Newbury Park: Sage.

Pheterson, Gail (ed). 1989. *A Vindication of the Rights of Whores*. Seattle: Seal Press.

Rainwater, Lee and William Yancy. 1967. *The Moynihan Report and the Politics of Controversy—A Transaction Social Science and Public Policy Report* Cambridge: M.I.T. Press.

Rapp, Rayna. 1987. "Urban Kinship in Contemporary America: Families, Class and Ideology." In *Cities of the United States: Studies in Urban Anthropology*, edited by Leith Mullings. New York: Columbia University.

Rios, Elsa. 1985. "Double Jeopardy: Cultural and Systemic Barriers Facing the Latina Battered Woman." Paper presented at the National Coalition Against Domestic Violence Conference, Seattle, WA. August, 1985.

Rollins, Judith. 1985. *Between Women: Domestics and Their Employers*. Philadelphia: Temple University.

Rosenbaum, Marsha. 1981. *Women on Heroin*. New Brunswick: Rutgers University.

Rubin, Lillian. 1976. *Worlds of Pain: Life in the Working-Class Family*. New York: Basic Books.

Russell, Diana. 1982. *Rape in Marriage*. Bloomington, IN: Indiana University.

Sacks, Karen. 1983. "Engels Revisited: Women, The Organization of Production and Private Property." In *Family in Transition: Rethinking Marriage, Sexuality, Child Rearing, and Family Organization*, edited by A. Skolnicka and J. Skolnick. New York: Little, Brown and Company.

Schechter, Susan. 1982. *Women and Male Violence: The Visions and Struggles of the Battered Women's Movement*. Boston: South End Press.

Scheff, Thomas. 1988. "Shame and Conformity: The Deference-emotion System." *American Socioloical Review*. 53:395-406.

Schott, Susan. 1979. "The Sociology of Emotions: Some Starting

Points." In *Theoretical Perspectives in Sociology*, edited by S. McNall. New York: St. Martin's Press.

Schur, Edwin. 1984. *Labeling Women Deviant: Gender, Stigma and Social Control*. New York: Random House.

Schwartz, Howard and Jerry Jacobs. 1979. *Qualitative Sociology: A Method to the Madness*. New York: The Free Press.

Shemen, Nancy. 1980. "Anger and the Politics of Naming." In *Women and Language in Literature and Society*, edited by S. McConnell-Ginet, R. Bork and N. Burman. New York: Greenwood.

Shenson, Douglas, Nancy Dubler, and David Michaels. 1990. "Jails and Prisons: The New Asylums?" *American Journal of Public Health*. 80:655-56.

Simons, Ronald and Les B. Whitbeck. 1991. "Sexual Abuse as a Precursor to Prostitution and Victimization Among Adolescent and Adult Homeless Women." *Journal of Family issues*. 12:3,361-79.

Smith, Dorothy E. 1987. *The Everyday World as Problematic: A Feminist Sociology*. Boston: Northeastern University.

Spunt, Barry, and Paul J. Goldstein, Patricia A. Bellucci, and Thomas Miller. 1990. "Race/Ethnicity and Gender Differences in the Drugs-Violence Relationship" *Journal of Psychoactive Drugs*. 22:3, 293-303.

Stack, Carol. 1974. *All Our Kin: Strategies for Survival in the Black Community*. New York: Harper and Row.

Stanko, Elizabeth. 1985. *Intimate Intrusions: Women's Experience of Male Violence*. London: Routledge and Kegan Paul.

Staples, Robert (ed). 1978. *The Black Family: Essays and Studies*. 2nd edition. Belmont, CA: Wadworth Publishing Co.

Staples, Robert. 1985. "Changes in Black Family Structure: The Conflict between Family Ideology and Structural Conditions." *Journal of Marriage and the Family*. 47:1005-1015.

Stark, Evan, Ann Flitcraft and William Frazier. 1977. "Medicine and Patriarchal Violence: The Social Construction of a 'Private Event'." *International Journal of Health Services* 9(3):461-94.

Straus, Murray Arnold and Richard J. Gelles. 1986. "Societal Change and Change in Family Violence from 1975 to 1985 as

Revealed by Two National Surveys." *Journal of Marriage and the Family*. 48:465-79.

Straus, Murray Arnold and Richard J. Gelles. 1990. *Physical Violence in American Families: Risk Factors and Adaptations to Violence in 8,145 Families*. New Brunswick: Transaction Publications.

Strauss, Anselm L. 1990. *Qualitative Analysis for Social Scientists*. San Francisco: University of California.

Sudarkasa, Niara. 1981. "African Heritage in Afro-American Family Organization." In *Black Families*, edited by H.P. McAdoo. Beverly Hills: Sage, 1981.

Taylor, Steven and Robert Bogdan. 1984. *Introduction to Qualitative Research*. New York: Wiley.

Thoits, Peggy. 1989 "The Sociology of Emotions." *Annual Review of Sociology*. 15:371-42.

Walker, Lenore. 1989. *Terrifying Love: Why Battered Women Kill and How Society Responds*. New York: Harper and Row.

Ward, E., M. Jackson and R. Ward. 1986. "Crime and Violence by Women." In *Crimes of Violence, President's Commission on Law Enforcement and Administrative Justice*. Washington, DC: U.S. Government Printing Office.

Watson, Lawrence and Maria-Barbara Watson-Franke. 1985. *Interpreting Life Histories*. New Brunswick: Rutgers University.

West, Candace and Don Zimmerman. 1987. "Doing Gender." *Gender and Society*. 1:2, 125-51.

Westen, Drew. 1985. *Self and Society: Narcissism, Collectivism and the Development of Morals*. New York: Cambridge University.

White, Evelyn. 1985. *Chain, Chain, Change for Black Women Dealing with Physical and Emotional Abuse*. Seattle: The Seal Press.

Wilson, William Julius. 1987. *The Truly Disadvantaged: The Inner City, The Underclass and Public Policy*. Chicago: University of Chicago.

Winch, Robert. 1972. "Theorizing About the Family." *Journal of Comparative Family Studies*. 3(1)5-16.

Yllo, Kristin and Michele Bograd. 1988. "Political and Methodological Debates in Wife Abuse Research." In *Feminist Perspectives on Wife Abuse,* edited by K. Yllo and M. Bograd. Newbury Park: Sage.

Zaretsky, Eli. 1986. *Capitalism, The Family and Personal Life.* New York: Perennial Library.

INDEX

abuse, in adulthood, 144
  arrest to avoid, 130
  emotional, 85-89
  physical results of, 82-84
  and pregnancy, 83-84
  psychological, 22
  vulnerability to, 70-80
  See also children, death of;
  violence
abuse, in childhood
  of battered African American
  women, 47-49, 65
  of battered white women, 50-
  51, 65
  of non-battered African Ameri
  can women, 49-50, 65
addiction. *See* drugs, use of
African American men, 162-163
African American women, battered
  gender-identity development of,
  33-36, 38-42, 47-49, 52-57, 59,
  61-62, 67-68
  paths to crime of, 102-103, 106-

125, 127-130
  and violence, 70-78, 80-84, 86-
  98, 140-147
African American women, non-
battered
  gender-identity development of,
  36-39, 43, 49-50, 54-55, 57-60,
  62, 64-68
  paths to crime of, 103-104, 123,
  125-126, 130
  and violence, 78-80, 140-147
agency, 161
All Our Kin (Stack), 17
anger, projection of, 110-114
anti-violence movement, 10-13
arrests, 6
  to avoid abuse, 130
assault, 22, 118-119
  See also violence, against women

Between Women (Rollins), 17

CPSIA information can be obtained at www.ICGtesting.com
Printed in the USA
LVOW092347070812

293312LV00006B/62/P